**Institutional
investing**

Institutional
investing

CHARLES D. ELLIS

Vice president
Donaldson, Lufkin & Jenrette, Inc.

1971
DOW JONES-IRWIN, INC.
HOMEWOOD, ILLINOIS 60430

First Printing, October, 1971
Second Printing, February, 1972

Library of Congress Catalog Card No. 76–168300
Printed in the United States of America

Bunny—
You're terrific

Preface

THIS BOOK seeks to organize and integrate into coherent form the most useful concepts, programs, and techniques developed by professional investment managers in recent years. I have borrowed widely and intensively from my partners, colleagues, clients, and competitors with whom I have enjoyed close personal and business relations, so in a real sense this book is a report on the present "state of the art" of institutional investing.

The text is designed to meet the common needs of several groups. The first consists of the several thousand individuals who are professional investors; they are the business analysts and portfolio managers who manage mutual funds, trust companies, brokerage firms, and pension and endowment funds, and advise wealthy private investors. Advanced students of business and finance who are preparing for careers in investments and related areas are a second group for whom this book is intended, and in the third group are the "clients" who must choose investment managers and set investment policies for pension funds, endowment funds, and other large pools of capital as well as for their own personal investments, whether large or small.

Readers will find no real attention given here to the oft-recited differences between various types of institutions such as mutual funds, trust companies, counselors, and endowment and pension fund managers. Their differences as investment institutions are not really due to legal differences, as is so often suggested, but rather arise from what might better be called cultural distinctions that have been reinforced by differences in the business strategies of the various institutions, which have in turn resulted in substantial differences in client expectations, decision structure, compensation and incentives, employee attitudes, work facilities, and so on, which have all in turn contributed to clearly different patterns of investment behavior. These behavioral differences have reinforced organizational differences so that over time each type of institutional investor has tended toward a refined or stereotyped form. But this "specialization" is not due to laws— man-made or divine—and is not necessary. There have always been the exceptions (the bank that operated like a mutual fund or the mutual fund that seemed bankish). Moreover, during the 1970s, as the various types of institutions enter the markets traditionally dominated by others, these parochial "differences" will probably fade. Consequently, the text concentrates on the major elements of investment management which are common to all these institutional investors.

The orientation of this book is toward decision making. Clear emphasis is given to the management of portfolios, as this is the decision center around which all other aspects of institutional investing must orbit. This book does not cover such specialized areas of investment management as venture capital, options, natural resources development, mortgages, or real estate. Nor does it deal with investment in foreign capital markets. And it does not delve into the fascinating potential of computer applications in investment management.

The objective is to provide serious readers with a profitable understanding of how the leading institutional investors are investing in equities and how the most productive investment methods can be adopted and adapted by the interested reader. This book should help the reader achieve superior investment results (including, hopefully, many of the professional investors whose ideas have contributed so much to it). Although the men and women who create, guide, and manage the better investment companies are imaginative, innovative, diligent, and shrewd, none of them has yet developed a perfect approach to institutional investing.

It would be impossible to give fair recognition to each of the individuals who have contributed to this book, but certainly my thanks go out to Susan Ellis, Bayard Hooper, Dean LeBaron, and Colyer Crum who read early drafts and gave many specific and useful suggestions for change.

I am deeply indebted to the financial editors who have helped me write (and forced me to rewrite) articles on investment management, portions of which have been used in this book: George J. W. Goodman, Peter Landau, and Heidi Fiske of *Institutional Investor,* Jack Treynor of *Financial Analysts Journal,* and David Ewing and Timothy Blodgett of *Harvard Business Review.* I prize their friendship.

My own personal thanks to Marie Flinn, Sylvia Takeuchi, Sharon Nearier, and Patricia Liddle who typed and retyped a book that was reworked more times than any of us would care to remember.

September, 1971   Charles D. Ellis
Douglaston, N.Y.

Contents

1

Introduction

INSTITUTIONAL investing is a new business; it is a phenomenon of the last two decades. Yet it is already a very big business with assets well in excess of $200 billion, and is growing nearly twice as fast as the national economy. This book is about institutional investing and how to achieve superior investment results for large, diversified equity portfolios. Specifically, this book is about "performance," because achieving superior investment performance for large pools of capital is what professional investing is all about.

Performance is the deliberate, regular, and predictable achievement of an agreed-upon investment objective whose long-term average rate of return is better than average returns available in the market because the portfolio either rises more than the market rises, or declines less than the market declines, or achieves some combination of both. "Performance" is not easy. But it can be accomplished, and this book seeks to explain how.

Before launching into our main themes, it seems appropriate to pause and make quite clear the kinds of investing that are *not* to be discussed here. First, we will not seriously

1

consider the overly defensive precepts of the outmoded investment advisers who were, or at least seemed to be, more concerned with the gentle art of client handholding than with the
demanding task of making capital more productive for its
owners.

Second, the problems of the individual amateur investor
are not of interest here, partly because many texts have been
written about his or her circumstances, but primarily because the part-time amateur is obsolete in today's professional market. (See Chapter 19.)

Finally, we are not concerned with stock market operations
that are included in "go-go" investing. This overly intensive
approach to investment management concentrates entirely
upon stock price behavior rather than growing value and is
much less concerned with the long-term causes than with the
near-term effects on share prices. *Price* is everything. The determination of *value* is not of interest. Swiftness of action,
particularly when fleeing adversity, is used as an alternative
to developing the longer term confidence that comes from
careful thought and study.

This does not mean that very aggressive investors serve no
purpose. The speculative fund managers are unabashedly
opportunistic and iconoclastic, and they distress traditionalists
who seem to find a lack of the dignified bearing they feel is
requisite to managers of investment capital. Such a simplistic
pejorative view would not be wise. These very aggressive investors are fulfilling the customary and generally desirable
role of informed speculation. But their techniques are not
sufficiently powerful to overcome the inherent inertia of a
large portfolio and propel it for sustained periods at satisfactory rates of return. This type of portfolio management is
too nearly trading and therefore too dependent upon an unusually artful operator's own instincts to be the subject of
serious study here.

Rejecting the lightweight, high-compression engine of the speculating "go-go" manager does not in any way mean that poor profitability is acceptable. Fashion in women's clothing has elements of fad and of style. The same applies to investing. The problem with fads is that rapid obsolescence requires too frequent replacement. Rejecting the fads puts greater emphasis on the more lasting qualities of style. In the same way, our rejection of short-term techniques puts even greater importance on the long-term methods of portfolio management that concern us in the coming chapters.

One more pause for perspective before turning to the major themes of this book. Since our topic is the large institutional equity portfolio, it may be wise to reflect for a moment on the nature of our topic. Just how big is $500 million? This question is important because the typical portfolio with which we will be concerned is between $200 million and one billion dollars, and so $500 million is for us a middle size. $500,000,000.00 is very large indeed. Less than 200 industrial corporations in America have more assets. Only a few hundred companies are "worth" more in the stock market. No individual has anywhere near such an amount of liquid wealth. Yale University's endowment, after 200 years of accumulation, is no larger.

But *static* measures can only hint at the real size of such a portfolio because the funds to be discussed here will be unusually *dynamic*. And it is the *flow* rather than the *stock* of capital that is really large. A typical fund of this size would have purchases and sales each year of between $200 million and $600 million! As a result, the dollar-decisions made by the portfolio manager must be viewed in a different perspective. In this context, the investment portfolio manager is investing more money each year than all but 25 companies among *Fortune*'s 500. Or in the context of the market, if we assume the average price of a common stock is $50, such a portfolio could buy every single share traded in a typical 10-million-share day. What is perhaps most surprising is that funds of this size are not really unusual. Among the bank trust departments, mutual funds, public and private pension funds, insurance companies, investment counselors, brokers, and endowment funds, there are well over one thousand as large as this. And over the coming decade many, many more portfolios will join this league.

Another way to measure the half-billion-dollar portfolio is to measure the portfolio's manager. One way to do this is to assume that the responsibility of the fund manager is to enhance the annual profitability of the portfolio by, say, 2 percent more than would have been earned under an "ordinary" manager. This slight 2 percent increment would add up to $10 million by year end, which means that if the manager works a typical 40-hour week for 50 weeks a year, he is "worth" $5,000 per hour!

Clearly, the man who commits several hundred million dollars during the course of a single year is making a great many decisions. Necessarily he is deciding what data are important and what are not, what is relevant to his problems and what is not. He is deciding to buy or to sell many, many times. Even more often, he is deciding *not* to decide—deciding not to buy or not to sell.

The stock market in which he conducts his business is a uniquely turbulent environment which is continuously reacting to political, social, economic, cultural, business, and financial changes at home and abroad. For most people, complete responsibility for managing a large treasury of "other peoples' money" in the midst of such chaos would be intolerable. And superior performance would be impossible.

The requirements of the job of managing portfolios described above can only be met by entrepreneurs of unusual character. They are, in the view of Harvard's Professor David C. McClelland, men with an unusually high "need for achievement." For them, the discontinuities of the investment environment, the intensity of the competition, and the precision of the score keeping are all *advantages*. An appreciation of this factor is important to anyone who wants to understand what has happened in the investment field in recent years, because entrepreneurs with high achievement needs have caused many great changes as they displaced the custodial investment managers who had conducted the affairs of portfolio management during the 1930s, 1940s, and 1950s.

It is true that the equity management field has suffered a rather special "generation gap" because few able men and women entered the field in the three decades between the Great Crash and the Korean War, and then, in the late 1950s and the 1960s, a large number of young people chose careers in institutional investing with the result that very few professional investors are "middle aged." And while most of the younger group had the opportunity to earn the MBA degree or the equivalent, not all the older group had enjoyed the luxury of graduating from college. But, despite the sharp divisions between the two groups, the new entrants differ less in age and education than in motivation, orientation, and attitudes toward themselves and their work.

These investment entrepreneurs have developed new approaches to portfolio management, and are creating and building new entrepreneurial organizations which are rooted in and grow out of flexible, profit-oriented portfolio management. They will have a far wider and more important impact in the future as their organizations grow in ability, strength, and influence.

Briefly stated, the pursuit of sustained superior performance is the subject of this book. Hence, describing average investment results is important. (Obviously, descriptions of average portfolio profits are limited to the past so it may well

TABLE 1

Rates of return on investment in common stocks listed on the New York Stock Exchange with reinvestment of dividends*
(percent per annum compounded annually)

| | *Tax bracket* | | | | | |
| | *No tax* | | *$10,000 in 1960* | | *$50,000 in 1960* | |
Period	*Portfolio to portfolio (rate)*	*Portfolio to cash** (rate)*	*Portfolio to portfolio (rate)*	*Portfolio to cash** (rate)*	*Portfolio to portfolio (rate)*	*Portfolio to cash** (rate)*
1926–60	9.03	9.01	8.46	8.20	7.42	6.84
1926–29	20.40	20.28	20.40	20.28	20.35	19.44
1926–32	−16.49	−16.76	−16.49	−16.76	−16.51	−13.37
1926–40	2.39	2.35	2.37	2.38	2.22	2.38
1926–50	6.80	6.77	6.32	6.15	5.53	5.14
1929–32	−48.36	−48.73	−48.36	−48.73	−48.19	−40.65
1929–40	− 2.98	− 3.04	− 3.00	− 2.85	− 3.00	− 2.28
1929–50	4.88	4.84	4.31	4.16	3.52	3.21
1929–60	7.74	7.71	7.05	6.81	5.97	5.39
1932–40	21.11	20.99	21.08	20.68	20.63	19.36
1932–50	18.61	18.56	17.83	17.43	16.48	15.47
1932–60	17.39	17.35	16.52	16.18	14.98	14.12
1950–52	12.50	11.97	11.09	10.00	8.99	7.12
1950–54	17.93	17.65	16.55	15.32	14.36	11.64
1950–56	16.98	16.79	15.78	14.80	13.72	11.43
1950–58	16.50	16.36	15.41	14.55	13.43	11.37
1950–60	14.84	14.72	13.85	13.09	12.01	10.30
1955–56	6.44	5.37	5.67	4.56	3.98	2.80
1955–57	− 3.66	− 4.19	− 4.38	− 3.98	− 5.99	− 4.22
1955–58	13.02	12.62	12.23	11.10	10.48	8.24
1955–59	14.00	13.70	13.26	12.16	11.58	9.23
1955–60	11.20	10.95	10.48	9.62	8.88	7.20

* The data underlying this table have been exhaustively checked, and it is believed that any subsequent refinement or adjustment will do no more than change the second digit after any decimal.

** "Portfolio to cash" means the net return which would have been realized after paying commissions and taxes (if any) if the portfolio were sold at the end of any period.

Source: *Rates of Return on Investments in Common Stocks,* Lorie and Fisher, University of Chicago, 1964.

TABLE 2

Rates of change in value of investment in common stocks listed on the New York Stock Exchange, ignoring dividends*
(percent per annum compounded annually)

| | *Income class* | | | | | |
| | *Tax exempt* | | *$10,000 in 1960* | | *$50,000 in 1960* | |
Period	*Cash to portfolio†*	*Cash to cash‡*	*Cash to portfolio†*	*Cash to cash‡*	*Cash to portfolio†*	*Cash to cash‡*
1/26–12/60	3.9	3.8	3.9	3.6	4.0	3.3
1/26– 9/29	15.7	15.6	15.7	15.6	15.7	14.8
1/26– 6/32	−21.0	−21.2	−21.0	−21.2	−20.9	−17.8
1/26–12/40	− 2.8	− 2.9	− 2.8	− 2.8	− 2.7	− 2.4
1/26–12/50	1.3	1.3	1.4	1.2	1.5	1.1
9/29– 6/32	−51.5	−51.9	−51.5	−51.9	−51.3	−43.4
9/29–12/40	− 8.0	− 8.0	− 8.0	− 7.7	− 7.6	− 6.4
9/29–12/50	− .5	− .6	− .5	− .6	− .2	− .3
9/29–12/60	2.5	2.4	2.5	2.2	2.7	2.1
6/32–12/40	16.9	16.8	16.9	16.4	16.8	15.1
6/32–12/50	13.1	13.0	13.0	12.5	13.0	11.7
6/32–12/60	11.9	11.9	11.9	11.4	11.8	10.8
12/50–12/52	5.9	5.4	5.9	4.8	5.9	4.0
12/50–12/54	11.4	11.1	11.3	10.1	11.3	8.6
12/50–12/56	10.8	10.7	10.8	9.8	10.8	8.4
12/50–12/58	10.7	10.6	10.7	9.8	10.7	8.5
12/50–12/60	9.6	9.4	9.5	8.7	9.5	7.6
12/55–12/56	1.5	.4	1.4	.4	1.4	.2
12/55–12/57	− 8.3	− 8.8	− 8.3	− 7.9	− 8.3	− 6.6
12/55–12/58	8.0	7.6	8.0	6.9	8.0	5.8
12/55–12/59	9.3	9.0	9.3	8.2	9.3	6.9
12/55–12/60	6.7	6.5	6.7	5.8	6.7	5.0

* The data underlying this table have been exhaustively checked. We are confident that any subsequent refinement or adjustment will do more than change an occasional figure after the decimal point.

† "Cash-to-portfolio" means the net rate of change which would have been experienced after paying commissions and taxes (if any) on each transaction but continuing to hold the portfolio at the end of each period.

‡ "Cash-to-cash" means the net change which would have been experienced after paying commissions and taxes (if any) on each transaction including the sale of the portfolio at the end of each period.

Source: *Rates of Return on Investments in Common Stocks*, Lorie and Fisher, University of Chicago, 1964.

be inappropriate to assume past measures are suitable to future use, and extrapolations must be made only with great care.) Several studies of average historical results have been made, of which the most comprehensive and least biased was reported in 1964 by L. Fisher and J. H. Lorie at the University of Chicago. (See Tables 1 and 2 for the results of this study.) These results are the *average* of a vast number of portfolios which were made entirely random as to stocks selected and periods held. This highly sophisticated and uniquely precise study of investment opportunity is too often summarized: "Investment profits from common stocks over long periods of time average 9 percent."

This is a case of unfortunate oversimplification in several ways. First, the history of the last 50 years will not be repeated during the next 50 years, so investing and investment opportunity will surely be very different. Even more important, these long-term results assume no taxes on interim profits and no management expense. Moreover, in the present era of putting primary emphasis on appreciation profits, it seems worth noting that the bulk of the "9 percent" came from *dividends*, and their systematic reinvestment: without dividends included, the 1926 to 1960 average rate of return was only 3.8 percent (Table 2). Another observation that should be made on the results of this study is that average returns in one decade differed importantly from average returns in other decades as can be quickly seen in both tables. One last point is especially important: the study deals only with an abstraction of investment profit opportunity; it does not measure results actually achieved by actual portfolios. Thus, for example, the large portfolios with which this book is concerned could not have operated on the study's assumption that buying or selling large positions, even in quite thin markets, would not have affected the transaction price.

The "above average" results of good performance have not

often been achieved by large portfolios, but the assumption underlying this book is that the failure lies not necessarily in their size but rather can be traced to suboptimal operating methods, policies, and organization. The ambitious purpose of this book is to offer an approach to institutional investing that could lead to the achievement of sustained superior performance for these portfolios.

2

Organizing
for performance

Exciting changes have taken place in the field of investment management in the past decade. While the idea of
"performance investing" has captured the attention of both
individual and institutional investors, the basic assumption
of this book is that sustained investment success can and does
result only when the investing institution is well organized
for performance. And so, organizing for performance is the
subject of this early chapter.

Every year a few investment management "stars" capture
the imagination and interest of both Wall Street and Main
Street, but they seldom endure for long periods. Meanwhile,
other investment managers are turning in consistently good
results. And they achieve performance not because they are
superstars, but because they are competent people who are
well organized to achieve performance. In order to achieve
comparable performance, we must pay serious attention to
understanding how they are organized. Observers who argue
that better research and more astute portfolio management

10

are the only important sources of investment success have identified only part of the explanation. This chapter deals with the larger part of the iceberg.

In any business, and particularly in the investment management business, effective corporate strategy typically involves several phases: specify the long-term goals of the organization; identify the problems and opportunities presented by the business environment; determine the internal strengths and weaknesses of the enterprise; and then—develop policies that allow management to minimize external problems and offset internal weaknesses while capitalizing on internal strengths and exploiting external opportunities. In each of these phases, the most successful investment management organizations have achieved superior operating results because they have developed their corporate strategies with more imagination, realism, and vigor.

The primary objective of the most successful investment companies is to maximize the value of capital under management. Capital *productivity* (rather than capital *preservation*) dominates the structure and activities of the entire organization, and all the efforts of each individual are aimed directly at contributing to portfolio profit. While these investment managers naturally seek to increase the flow of new monies coming under their management, they concentrate on managing existing capital effectively on the assumption, more than validated in recent years, that if they excel with present funds, substantial new money will flow in. Thus, by achieving the portfolio profit-maximizing goal, the management group's earnings will rise as both capital gains and voluntary capital additions increase the amount of capital under management. Balancing this unswerving insistence on a single operating objective are a variety of highly pragmatic and flexible attitudes on principles that were formerly considered inviolate.

For example, contemporary concepts of investment management give full recognition to significant historical changes in the operating environment which lead to a redefinition of portfolio management. In contrast to "generally accepted investing principles," when describing what they are doing, portfolio managers often are quite blunt. Here are some examples: They begin with the truism that "a common stock is not a company." Portfolio managers say they "buy stocks"; they do not "invest in corporations." Their reasoning is that corporate management is really quite independent of investors because when a stock is purchased from or sold to another investor, no money flows into or out of the corporation. Consequently, the equity investor seldom can exercise any significant economic control over the future of any company in which he might own common shares, and so should be realistic enough to accept this situation as a "given."

In the view of these managers, a short-term orientation is wrong only if the long-term view is more profitable. Since market prices change frequently, holding a stock for a long time does not really avoid the risk of adverse daily, weekly, monthly, and yearly price changes, and prevents taking profitable advantage of these changes. If portfolio value is to be maximized in the long run, stocks must be owned when they are rising in price most rapidly and not owned when declining in price or even when they are not rising as rapidly as are other stocks.

To the new managers, one major advantage compensates for the uncertainty of frequent price changes and the lack of investor influence over corporate progress. This one major advantage is *liquidity*. As share prices change either absolutely or relative to other share prices, the liquidity of the stock market enables the aggressive portfolio manager to change his holdings whenever he believes he can improve the profit potential of the portfolio. Liquidity—the ease and speed with which portfolio holdings can be changed at a realistic price—is an important environmental opportunity to be used vigorously to maintain the profit vitality of the portfolio.

Another observation on the current investment environment is that opportunities for profitable changes in the portfolio have increased in number and magnitude because share prices have become more volatile in the past decade. Several factors underlie this development: increasing information disclosure by corporations and expanding broker research organizations have increased the depth and detail of available investment information; the speed of information dispersal and investor response to this information is more rapid; and the growth in aggressively managed institutional capital has multiplied the volume of insistent supply or demand which may come into the market and cause important changes in share prices.

Change and change in the *rate* of change are the only constants in the investment field, so the principal concern of the portfolio manager must be with possible and probable changes in prices and values which will offer the portfolio manager opportunities to profitably change his holdings. Of course, if a stock's value is primarily determined by dividend yield or by underlying assets, changes in either will affect price. And if price is a function of per share earnings, it can fail because of any of three causes: earnings decline; earnings rise, but less rapidly than expected; earnings rise, but earnings of other stocks rise more rapidly. And price can rise for the three reciprocal changes in earnings. The investment manager must of course be concerned with price, not in theory, not by categorical rules, nor by analytical convention, but in terms of the prices that will be realized in the stock market. Since the capital markets are not perfect, actual price will not always equal value and value will not always equal price, but understanding value is important because it helps the investment manager to understand prices and to anticipate price changes upon which he can capitalize.

The new approach to investment management deals in terms of the aggregate portfolio rather than solely with individual securities. This approach leads to several productive concepts. First, the portfolio should represent a strategy of resource deployment that is responsive to the total economic-business-social-market environment; individual security selection follows from the purpose developed for the portfolio as a whole. This "portfolio strategy" will be changed regularly in response to changes in the environment. Second, a security that is likely to underperform the overall portfolio is not tolerable. Holding a dull security prevents acquiring a more profitable resource for the portfolio and incurs an opportunity cost of profits foregone. Third, the long-term obligations of the portfolio do not require holding each constituent security for a long time, but rather depend upon continuously rearranging the composite so that at each point in time the portfolio's probable long-term value is maximized. This requires persistent investment and reinvestment to add value to the portfolio, often by what may seem quite modest individual increments. But these seemingly modest gains *do* add up.

Given this redefinition of portfolio management, the traditional investment company organizational structure has important weaknesses that can be reduced or eliminated by changes in management organization and method. Traditional investment management is oriented towards very long term investment decisions, relies on a committee of senior officers to make all investment action decisions at weekly or bimonthly meetings, depends primarily on a staff of in-house analysts for information and evaluation, and conducts its affairs in private. Since the principal investment objective is capital preservation, caution and conservatism tend to characterize the decision process. Unfortunately, in the dynamic arena of contemporary institutional investing, delay and defensive thinking can be very costly. More than in most fields, a strong offense is the best defense, and committees have great difficulty managing truly competitive portfolios.

In a very real sense, in the business of portfolio management, time *is* money, and the necessarily slow decision process of a committee can be very expensive to the portfolio. Memoranda prepared for committees take precious analytical time away from productive research efforts and delay actions, often until it is too late to act because prices have already changed. Profit opportunities provided by frequent market swings have to be ignored by a committee and only the very long term opportunities can be considered.

Committee decisions are not easily reversed (although market liquidity allows it) with the result that tentative, experimental purchases or sales are impossible even though most investment experts agree that the very best and most profitable ideas are almost always "soft-shelled," tentative thoughts that cannot survive being "kicked around" by a committee. Committee politics and investment creativity do not mix.

The portfolio manager can act much more quickly than a committee; he need not wait for a committee meeting. His decision process can be quite informal, avoiding the communications delays inherent in the preparation of a formal presentation of an investment recommendation. So, the new concept of capital management assigns both the authority and the responsibility for operating decisions to the portfolio manager. Like a product manager in a marketing company, he operates under a policy and review committee, but is fully responsible for making all operating decisions. The committee system, on the other hand, makes it very difficult to assign responsibility and to measure results: Who can take credit for good decisions? And who can be held accountable for poor decisions?

The competent individual has other advantages over a committee in making investment decisions. Since he devotes all his time and energies to the success of the portfolio, it stands to reason that he'll know more about each security—why it was bought, why it's held, and why it might be sold. Since portfolio management is more art than science, and since committees are notoriously not artful, the single portfolio executive who is personally skilled in this art will enjoy a significant competitive strength. He can also exploit his intuition, inventiveness, and sense of the market, because he is judged on overall results in the market place, *not* on how well he can explain, advocate, or document his individual actions. Since the portfolio manager is judged on the profitability of the portfolio as a whole, he is more clearly motivated to take sensible risks with individual securities where the rewards are commensurate. He can act boldly and seize the initiative to increase portfolio profits. In portfolio management, astute risk taking is well rewarded.

Since committees can only make a few decisions each meeting, their portfolios tend to be *managed by exception*, selling "bad" stocks and buying "good" ones. The new management wants portfolio *management by control* and recognizes that investment decisions are seldom clearly identified in blacks and whites, but rather appear in varying shades of gray which warrant frequent, almost continuous adaptation in the composition of the portfolio.

An individual investment manager working full time on the problems and opportunities facing his portfolio can exercise management by control. The logic is in the mathematics of time. A committee that meets 50 times a year for two-hour sessions cannot make as many decisions as an executive working 250 full days a year. The independent portfolio man-

ager's capacity to make more decisions enables him to be
more aggressive in his efforts to capture more increments of
profit for the portfolio.

Now this does not mean that investment committees do not
have any important functions in a modern investment management organization. A good investment committee should
make two important contributions. First, serious errors in
judgment seldom survive open review because a committee
composed of men with diverse attitudes and experience can
usually raise most potentially significant questions. A committee can often prove helpful as a review board concerned with whether actions taken fit properly with the
portfolio objective. The second contribution of an effective
committee is even more important: it can and should establish sound basic investment *policy*. But this does not mean
than the committee should also make such *operating* decisions as security selection, timing of transactions, or degree
of emphasis on individual securities. In fact, if the committee
attempts to run the portfolio, it will not only give too little
time and attention to its major responsibilities of policy setting and review, but will usually make inferior operating
decisions. So, the new managements clearly separate *policy*
decisions from *operating* decisions. A committee will typically set the objectives and review the specific actions taken
by the portfolio manager in pursuit of these objectives, but
the portfolio manager makes the "on-line" decisions himself.

Turning now to the research function, it is clear that the
successful investment management organizations strive not
only to be highly effective at making decisions, but also at
acquiring and evaluating the information upon which these
decisions must be based. The traditional approach to data
collection and appraisal relies upon a permanent private staff
of analysts who study statistics, visit managements, and write
reports recommending purchases and sales to the investment

committee. The research process is treated as proprietary and confidential, and is considered the sole responsibility of the in-house staff.

Today institutional investors are recognizing that while internal research is a valuable strength, it can also lead to a constriction on the flow of important information to the decision maker. External suppliers of investment information and judgment, particularly the brokerage firms who specialize in serving the needs of institutional investors, can and do make important contributions to the profitability of large portfolios. (The emergence of these research firms has been one of the most important changes in the investment field in recent years. Very few institutions have in-house research staffs equal in size or experience to the research departments of these firms which will often have 15 or 20 senior analysts with many assistants, large libraries, computers, and generous budgets for visiting managements and retaining expert consultants on technical subjects.)

The view that research-oriented brokerage firms can be of great value is coupled with a clear awareness of the service buying power of brokerage commissions generated in the normal management of a large portfolio. Large investment institutions will usually generate several millions of dollars of brokerage commissions each year, and by executing portfolio transactions through brokerage firms that provide research, the investment managers can attract the best research analysts and apply their best thinking to the needs and opportunities of that portfolio. This commission buying-power should be managed carefully, and deliberately expended to acquire research and judgment from brokers which will add the most value to the portfolio.

Another major innovation in capital management is apparent in the way in which brokers' research is integrated into the investment management process, again showing how new organizational concepts reflect careful evaluation of internal strengths and weaknesses. Recognizing that a communications gap can develop between the operating needs of the institutional portfolio manager and the growing store of research knowledge and security valuation capabilities of research oriented brokers, and realizing that effectively bridging this communications gap can gain for them a competitive advantage over other institutional managers, more and more institutions are treating research brokers as part of the portfolio management team, and are working more and more closely together. Whereas the traditional investment managements insist that all broker research go only to the staff analysts, the new approach often channels this valuable information and opinion flow directly to the portfolio manager.

This practice derives from an appreciation of subtle human differences between analyst and portfolio manager, their position within the organization, and how they respond to external opinion. Staff analysts often are not very well suited to appreciating the merits of the "outside" analysts' recommendations for many reasons. A good analyst is necessarily skeptical and tends to discount what others say; he distrusts and disparages relying on the work of others; he knows too much about "his" stocks to be impressed by a summary description of other securities; his professional satisfaction often depends more on the breadth and depth of his factual company and industry knowledge than on the profitability of portfolio purchase and sale decisions; his career development typically depends more upon the consistent accuracy of his research reports than upon the frequency and magnitude of his contributions to the portfolio's profitability. He makes far fewer recommendations each year than a portfolio manager makes decisions, and so has a smaller set of commitments over which to obtain a satisfactory average of profitability. And he has less opportunity to reverse decisions, so he must realistically be more confident of each individual security endorsement. Staff analysts usually build their reputations on percentage profits, not dollar profits; they do better professionally when a small stock triples than when a large holding goes up 30 or 40 percent, so they naturally tend to concentrate on small stocks. Besides, it's more fun to discover an exciting new company than to reappraise a well-known and well-established corporation. For all these reasons, a staff analyst often is ill-suited by position, responsibility, and interest to effectively exploit the research supplied by institutional brokers.

In contrast, the portfolio manager must always rely heavily on the knowledge and appraisals of others, whether they be internal staff analysts or external broker-analysts. He must be just as receptive to one analyst as he is to another if they can equally increase the profits of the portfolio. His primary skill is in seeing the positive potential in a situation rather than in identifying possible negatives. He thinks in terms of stock prices and relative value rather than absolute value, and works with stocks in a shifting market context rather than with isolated companies. Consequently, the contemporary management philosophy offers the portfolio manager wide access to ideas and information upon which he can act quickly, or which he may pass on to a staff analyst for evaluation if he is interested but not yet convinced that action should be taken now.

A second way to deal with the natural tendency for staff analysts to have a separate orientation from that of the portfolio manager is to recast their role so that each analyst sees himself as an assistant portfolio manager rather than a staff specialist. He is expected to concentrate his efforts on flowing profit-making ideas into the portfolio. In this new role analysts more readily see outside research as an advantageous opportunity to save their time, broaden their knowledge, cover

more investment opportunities, and increase their profit contribution to the portfolio, and will therefore more readily use
the information and opinions of others. They will build upon
the work of these external analysts and sort out the best thinking of several experts rather than recreating the original research, with the strong probability that their value added to
the portfolio will be greater than if time, efforts, and talents
were devoted to independent original research.

One aspect of the traditional organization of the investment
community that has been adopted by the new managers, apparently without seriously questioning it, seems peculiar. The
principal intermediary between institutional brokers' research
and portfolio managers' decisions is employed by the brokerage firm. Why is this individual not employed by the investment firm as an assistant to the portfolio manager? This is
the role towards which the in-house research staff should be
moving since a very few men could easily cover the most
productive research brokers on a regular and intensive basis.
And knowing quite clearly what the portfolio manager is
concerned with on a day-to-day basis, these men could concentrate on gathering desired data and opinion while pro-
tecting the portfolio decision maker from a barrage of not
relevant ideas, facts, and suggestions. Perhaps this will come
with time.

Another way of looking at the value of broker research is
to think of the 15 or 20 firms that an institutional investor
will usually work with as a diversified portfolio of information sources. All together, these firms will have over 200
senior analysts, of whom perhaps six or eight will be experts
on the automobile industry and the companies in it. The
institutional portfolio manager who wants to evaluate Chrysler can get several different expert views of the company, its
competitors, suppliers, and markets; can cross check the
different analysts' reports to separate hard fact from interpre-

tation; and can ask the various experts to evaluate for him the opinions of the other experts. He can get the same advantages that President Roosevelt sought from his staff by asking several experts to study the same question so he could decide the basic issues for himself, free of the biases that any adviser brings with him to questions of evaluation and judgment. In addition, while an individual analyst may visit the Chrysler management only once a quarter, the half dozen broker-analysts will, as a group, visit management every few weeks and so can provide the fund manager virtually continuous information.

Since investment information is useful only if it contributes to the profitability of the portfolio, the fund manager must be actively involved in the acquisition, processing, and use of available information. An effective data network is a complex thing that requires planning and husbandry. Two phases are primary: acquiring as much useful information as possible, and screening out as much unnecessary data as quickly as possible. Clearly, efforts in one direction can conflict with efforts in the other direction, and tradeoffs must be made. The purpose of organization and procedure in the information handling system is to reduce the conflicts and avoid stultifying compromises between seeking all the relevant information and getting inundated with trivia. There is no "one right way" solution to this problem, but each investment manager should strive to develop an information system that works well for him.

The portfolio manager must balance two other competing demands—that he make as many decisions as possible, and that each decision be as good or as profitable as possible. The accompanying graph shows the nature of this tradeoff with the vertical axis representing the *quality* of the individual decisions and the horizontal axis representing the *quantity* of decisions made. The curves indicate the tradeoff between the two. The challenge is to find an information-action system that puts the portfolio manager on the curve farthest away from the origin and at the optimal point on that curve. This, too, is easier said than done, but defining the problem is an important and necessary step towards solving it.

The new concept of investment management includes a healthy respect for the open market as the arena within which management effectiveness will be demonstrated or denied. Since every stock purchase or sale decision is made in terms of market price expectations, fund managers seriously study the market behavior of individual stocks, industry groups, and even larger aggregates. Supply and demand for equities, significant correlations between the market and various economic indicators, and the investment actions of other large investors are studied because their actions can and do affect stock prices. Trading expertise and skill are seen as an opportunity to obtain better long-term profits for the portfolio by minimizing transaction costs. Responsibility for executing orders is usually assigned to one member of the management team who works full time in this area. Because the institutional trader is constantly involved with the market, he often has insights into the structure of supply and demand for individual stocks and groups of stocks that are likely to determine near-term prices, and is often able to contribute to the profit-maximizing goal by advising the portfolio manager on timing of transactions and on unusual opportunities to buy or sell created by temporary imbalances of supply and demand in the market. In addition, the trader should develop the personal and business relations with the brokers who have developed the ability to execute large "block trades" quickly and at favorable prices so the portfolio can be redeployed in more attractive stocks. An important aspect of the traders' role is to be able to call upon the unusual liquidity that can be obtained from those few institutional brokers who make "position bids" for blocks of stocks and will put their own capital at risk to buy quite large amounts of stock when the market will not immediately absorb a large supply of shares. The importance of developing these relationships with leading "block brokers" has been demonstrated in many ways. For example, one large institutional investor—with the help of a leading brokerage firm—was able to sell nearly $100 million of thinly traded stocks in 25 different life insurance companies in just two days without affecting the normal 100 share over the counter market prices of these issued. (Even the market for U.S. Treasury Bills would be affected by that kind of volume!) In another case, this same firm agreed to buy with its own capital over $20 million of one stock that a large, well-informed institution wanted to sell swiftly. This extraordinary kind of liquidity—who could seriously expect to sell $20 million of real estate with a single telephone call? —can be essential to aggressive, institutional investing. But it will only be provided to those institutions who work closely with the "block brokers," so the new approach to institutional portfolio management makes sure this "escape hatch" is available in case of need.

Finally, the management goal of portfolio profitability is supported by the incentives provided to individual members of the management organization. Pay tends to be closely related to an individual's ability to contribute to portfolio profitability. The most important job in terms of income, professional responsibility, prestige, and influence is that of portfolio manager. (The business management and administration of the organization are separated from the investment function in much the same way broadcasters separate programming from time sales and newspapers and magazines separate editorial from business. Very few people are able to excel in such different areas of activity; virtually none have been successful in both areas simultaneously.)

The personal, nonfinancial incentives are also important in these free-form, multiprofit-center managements in which each person functions as an entrepreneur; and ability to contribute to portfolio profitability is quickly recognized and quickly rewarded. As in most fields of organized endeavor, the essential ingredient for sustained superior results is the ability and effectiveness of the people in management, and the new concept of capital management has emphasized the importance of profit-making people. While the most successful investment managers often differ significantly in their approach to investing—particularly the kinds of securities they use and the ways they use them—these managers are all similar in this one most important way: their goals and methods and organization are all carefully, purposefully, and deliberately balanced and mutually consistent. And in each case, they specialize in one—and only one—of the many ways in which investment performance can be achieved. Having selected their investment approach, they practice and practice and practice with it; they eschew tempting distractions that are out of harmony with their own long-run, continuing program; they develop procedures and recruit people who will strengthen their hands in this most important game. Coordination and specialization are the common denominators of effective investment management organizations.

In conclusion, observation of the investment records of a still small but rapidly growing number of effective capital management groups gives compelling evidence that their superior achievements are due to a clearer understanding of their working environment, their organizational goal, their internal strengths and weaknesses as well as the strengths and weaknesses of their competitors, and the policies and practices that will enable them to minimize problems and exploit opportunities so as to more fully realize the goal of portfolio profit maximization. In brief, they achieve superior investment performance because they are organized for performance.

3

Policy in portfolio
management: Bonds

BEHIND the discussion of portfolio management in this chapter and the three following chapters is a conviction that a well-managed portfolio will not be evenly diversified; it should and will have bulges, imbalances, and irregularities. Moreover, these intentionally prominent features will regularly be rebuilt to new designs as investment opportunities change. A well-developed portfolio will quite clearly reveal the manager's philosophy and his expectations. The portfolio will have structure and momentum such that another professional portfolio manager will be able to "read the plan of battle." If there are no plot and no leading character roles, the individual security holdings are no more a portfolio than talk is drama.

This chapter focuses on Policy as one of the three ways of building prominent investment characteristics into a large portfolio of common stocks. Briefly, the three phases of portfolio management are: *Policy*, which sets the long-term posture of the portfolio towards the capital markets as markets;

27

Strategy, which is concerned with the changing economic environment and ways to identify major areas of investment opportunity within the market; and *Selection,* which deals with buying and selling specific securities at specific times. Portfolio management can and should be conducted on each of these planes simultaneously.

When formulating long-term policy for large institutional portfolios, it is important to avoid one enticing temptation. The history of the capital markets shows those of us with 20–20 hindsight numerous opportunities to make truly enormous profits by "catching" the major turns—switching from stocks to bonds in 1928 and going back to stocks in 1948. Most experienced investors would agree that these admittedly major opportunities are virtually impossible to see at the time and that trying to exploit them usually involves many false—and costly—starts. Changing policy in response to short-term expectations seldom augments long-term portfolio profits. The risk of suffering large losses, trying to switch from one policy to another and back again later, was amply demonstrated in the poor results of the ill-fated Yale and Vassar plans which involved elaborate decision rules that were expected to swing their endowment funds back and forth between bonds and stocks at just the right times. The result in both cases was wholesale selling of stocks in the late forties— just as the biggest bull stock market in history was gathering momentum. And the proceeds were put into bonds just before a major bear market in bonds! Policy alternatives should be carefully weighed, deliberately chosen, and held to for prolonged periods. If policy is well developed, it will have long-term validity.

Policy's three market alternatives are cash, bonds, and stocks. In this chapter, the focus is on bonds, and the basic question is this: Should a truly long-term institutional portfolio have a long-term investment in bonds? This may seem at first to be a curious question whose only answer is "Of course." But can we develop a persuasive, logical argument in favor of sustained, long-term investment in bonds that would explain satisfactorily why the custodians of almost every pension fund, endowment fund, and large personal trust in the nation have owned, now hold, and plan to continue investing in long-term corporate and government bonds with a major portion of their funds?

It seems appropriate to question the wisdom of this policy for large, long-term investment portfolios. Proponents of long-term, continuous investment in bonds in large institutional portfolios argue four main propositions:

1) Preservation of principal is assured because at maturity the bond must be repaid in full.

2) The yield on bonds is typically higher than common stock yields and the extra income is often needed now, and interest income from bonds is assured as to amount and time of payment.

3) If the national economy should suffer a severe and prolonged depression, bonds would once again prove very valuable protection against serious trouble.

4) Trustees of pension funds, trusts, and endowments are bound by the Prudent Man Rule of fiduciary obligation to invest in bonds to have a balanced portfolio.

Let's analyze these propositions carefully, taking them in reverse order, beginning with the fourth. The Prudent Man Rule governing the duty of a trustee in the Commonwealth of Massachusetts, and now recognized quite widely, states: "He is to observe how men of prudence, discretion and intelligence manage their own affairs, not in regard to speculation but in regard to the permanent disposition of their funds, considering the probable income as well as the probable safety of the capital to be invested." In the past, prudent men bought and held bonds in their personal portfolios, but today, sophisticated investors do not buy bonds and hold them for the long term. (Municipal bond holdings of wealthy individuals are a function of the tax incentive without which these investors would not be bond buyers. From time to time, investors will buy long-term bonds in anticipation of capital gains due to a change in interest rates, but this is essentially speculation as they do not intend to hold the bonds for the long term. These two exceptions to the basic statement about owning bonds are just that—exceptions.)

Perhaps the reason bonds are held in most institutional portfolios is just a holdover of a portfolio policy that may have been well enough suited to personal trust and estate problems without being carefully reevaluated to identify the important differences between the investment problems and responsibilities of estate planners and those of very long-term institutional portfolios. While such an explanation is possible, it would be imprudent to let it go unchallenged. Trust management is historically based on experience in managing the financial affairs of mortal men who unfortunately do not live very long. The investment manager of a personal trust that will not last forever and is subject to an uncertain date of termination may well emphasize conservation of capital for the individual's descendents while planning for an estate settlement and portfolio liquidation.

In contrast, endowments, pension funds, mutual funds, and insurance companies have one unique and distinguishing characteristic: they will continue for very long, virtually indefinite periods. An endowment has an unusually long-term obligation to finance all or at least a considerable portion of the activities of a presumably very long lived organization or institution. A pension fund also has a long-term obligation to provide for the well-being of many workers during their retirement. And even most personal funds will be looked to for such long-term needs as education, retirement, and family security. These cannot be bound by the rules of estate planning because those rules give no explicit attention to the growth of capital and income which any growing institution would naturally seek from its endowment, which any corporation would expect of pension fund investments, and which any individual expects of his capital. (Since "prudent men" looking to their own affairs generally avoid bonds, perhaps the rule would then forbid investing in bonds.) Rules, particularly those formed for different times, must not be accepted blindly, so let us analyze the more substantial parts of the bond-partisans' view.

With regard to the third pro-bond argument cited above, the risk of a major economic depression, a powerful case can be built to support the view that, excluding an externally caused calamity such as a major world war, this nation should suffer neither severe nor prolonged economic setbacks such as occurred in the 1930s. Students of economic history can specify a myriad of statistics to show how different our economic position is today in comparison to the twenties and thirties. High and widespread personal incomes provide economic stability, while research, technology, and education provide growth. Again, the high proportion of workers in services and white-collar jobs reduces economic cyclicality, while large investments in plant and equipment per worker support economic growth. Meanwhile, political scientists will point to the important institutional changes that have so greatly changed our economic structure such as FHA and VA loan guarantees, FDIC bank deposit insurance, IMF reserves, unemployment compensation, Social Security, progressive taxation, enormous government spending at federal, state, and local levels, the SEC, FPC, FCC, and other regulatory agencies, pension funding, and particularly the Employment Act of 1946 which placed direct responsibility for economic growth, price stability, and low unemployment with the federal government. These objectives have been reinforced by the commitment of recent presidents to fulfill this federal economic obligation. Ours is a greatly different economy from the economy of our fathers and grandfathers, and long-term investment policy should be commensurately different.

Perhaps the most favorable change over the past 40 years is that our economy is now a managed economy, and managed rather well both by government officials and by businessmen. Business managers have gained substantial control over the uncertainties which have in the past caused large fluctuations in inventories and capital spending—which have in turn been the major progenitors of past business cycles. And the federal government has learned a great deal about the effective uses of fiscal and monetary policy to guide the economy away from rampant inflation on the one hand and away from accelerating declines on the other hand. (The Vietnam war has proven a serious economic hazard, but without major sacrifices by our citizens, we are weathering the storm tolerably well—far better than could reasonably have been expected in 1920 or 1940.) The public and private managers of our economy are equipped with more voluminous, accurate, and timely data than could have been imagined just a few decades ago. The development of computers and the advent of econometric model building have made forecasting, analysis, and evaluation increasingly rapid and reliable. We are steadily gaining a sound understanding of the way a complex industrial-service economy operates and how effective management can avoid serious imbalances and beneficially influence development. This is not intended to suggest that we live in a "new era" from which recession and inflation are banished, but it does seem highly probable that we do not face the prospect of either prolonged or severe economic depression. Consequently, no major portion of long-term portfolios should be aimed at defending against the remote prospect of sustained economic adversity when such a defensive posture means sacrificing the opportunity to invest more positively in the nearly continuous growth of our dynamic economy.

This positive outlook does not deny the remote possibility of unforeseen economic, business, or investment adversities that could reduce current investment income, and a contingency reserve may be desirable. If so, this protection should be provided by a small part of the total assets and held in highly liquid form—from which it could be withdrawn for current spending when and if needed—rather than by allocating 30, 40, or 60 percent of the total fund to bonds for protection against a decline in investment income which may not develop and which is highly uncertain as to timing.

Using a small, "fully spendable" reserve means that the degree of protection or insurance against a drop in income needed by most large and long-term portfolios can be accomplished in most cases with a reserve only 5 to 10 percent of the portfolio. For example, a large appliance manufacturer has a continuing special reserve set aside within its pension fund. Management has already agreed to spend this reserve at any time that current investment income plus company contributions are not large enough to meet pension benefit obligations. And with that concern satisfied, the rest of the fund is available for profit-maximizing investment. On the other hand, a large portfolio of bonds would incur too great an opportunity cost in investment profits foregone, as will be shown below, to warrant using large holdings of bonds as massive insurance against unlikely and uncertain adversity.

The remaining pro-bond propositions—assurance of income at a high level and capital preservation—are the key investment considerations and can be tested by comparing a portfolio of long-term bonds with a conservative portfolio of, say, utility common stocks represented by Moody's Utility

Average. In questioning the long-term financial validity of bond investments for long-term portfolios, we will use ten-year time periods as the basis for evaluating bonds and the equity alternative. This test period is only for analytical convenience, and the reader should keep in mind that ten years is only a very short term "proxy" for the truly long term character of the funds with which we are primarily concerned.

Turning now to the bond advocates' proposition two, and comparing cash income from bond interest to cash income from utility common stock dividends, the record presented in Table 3 shows that in all but one ten-year period since World

TABLE 3

Ten-year cash income per $1,000 investment

Period	Interest on bond portfolio	Dividends on utility portfolio
1945–54	$267	$656
1946–55	258	534
1947–56	267	646
1948–57	292	729
1949–58	276	709
1950–59	268	696
1951–60	295	694
1952–61	305	662
1953–62	332	653
1954–63	300	584
1955–64	313	551
1956–65	343	581
1957–66	403	512
1958–67	392	446
1959–68	456	419
1960–69	453	514

War II, total cash income from a portfolio of utility common stocks purchased in the first year and held for ten years, exceeded the income from long-term Aa utility bonds bought in that same first year. On average, over a ten-year span,

Moody's utility dividends returned 6.4 percent on cost versus a peak yield of 4.6 percent for the bonds, or an average increase in income earned of 40 percent.

Over longer periods, the advantage of equities increases substantially. On a pure rate of return basis, a dividend yielding 4 percent currently and growing at 6 percent annually earns as much cash income over a 20-year period as a bond yielding 6.5 percent. And over even longer periods, the algebra is exorable. What bond could compete for very long with an equity portfolio that currently yields 4 percent and is growing at 6 percent? This means the dividend income would double every 12 years producing 8 percent on cost in 12 years, 16 percent on cost in 24 years, 32 percent in 36 years, and, to carry the proposition to a century time span, which will really test our capacity to think in truly long terms, the dividend would yield 1,024 percent in the 96th year!

Granted that dividends of conservative common stocks have yielded and are expected to yield more cash income over long periods, are not bond interest receipts more predictable? It is quite clear that the amount of dividends to be received from specific stocks over a period of many years cannot be forecast exactly, but the very probable rate of growth in earnings of a portfolio of seasoned equities can be translated into a highly probable pattern of dividends. And although the pattern of dividend income would be less assured than the pattern of income received on a specific present portfolio of bonds, just the *reverse* would be true for a large, continuing, and therefore always changing, portfolio of bonds. For while we know precisely what interest will be paid on what dates for each individual bond now owned, most issues in any present portfolio will have matured or been called in 20 years and will be replaced with other bonds paying interest rates that are presently unknown. Viewed in this long-term perspective, a bond portfolio's income would be expected to be not *more*, but *less* certain than the income from a portfolio of conservative common stocks because we do not know whether bond yields will trend higher or lower, whereas the common stock portfolio's dividend income will almost surely trend higher, and only the rate of increase is uncertain.

The essential conclusion is that while the yield of the present bond portfolio is highly certain, the yield of a future bond portfolio cannot be accurately predicted and is less predictable than the future yield on cost of a conservative common stock portfolio. The evidence substantiates this view. While interest rates have declined nine times on a year-to-year basis during the past two decades, common stock dividends for Moody's Utility Average never once declined in the postwar period. Thus, the utility portfolio provides not only a higher, but also a steadier, more predictable stream of current income than a bond portfolio.

While this discussion of the very long term advantages of common stocks over bonds has been based on a portfolio of electric utility stocks, portfolio managers can and should consider a far broader list of equities. A review of total corporate earnings and dividends indicates quite dramatically that while aggregate dividends rise with increasing earnings, dividends generally do not fall when earnings drop during business recessions (see Table 4). Thus, in the 20 years since World War II, total corporate dividends have declined on a year-to-year basis only once—by a mere 2.3 percent in 1952. Yet, during that same 20-year period dividends rose by nearly 300 percent or at an average annual rate of 7.2 percent compounded. On the record, bonds are clearly inferior as a source of reliable income when compared to equities.

Regarding proposition four, which discusses capital, its preservation and conservation, it is curious that advocates of bond investment appear so convinced that the contractual nature of a bond is always an advantage to the bond buyer.

TABLE 4

**Cash payments on common stocks
(millions of dollars)**

Calendar year	Estimated aggregate payments	Calendar year	Estimated aggregate payments
1929	2,711	1958	8,711
1930	2,667	1959	9,337
1935	1,336	1960	9,872
1940	2,099	1961	10,430
1945	2,275	1962	11,203
1950	5,404	1963	12,096
1951	5,467	1964	13,555
1952	5,595	1965	15,302
1953	5,874	1966	16,151
1954	6,439	1967	16,866
1955	7,488	1968	18,124
1956	8,341	1969	19,404
1957	8,807		

Source: New York Stock Exchange, *Fact Book*, 1970.

Granted that the contract protects the investor from receiving *less* than stipulated, it also prohibits the investor from receiving any *more*. This situation can be viewed as a source of risk when we consider inflation's erosion of the future purchasing power of both income and capital. In fact, if inflation continues at the long-term historical rate of 2 percent, the assurance that a bond buyer will only recover at maturity the dollars he puts up, is the assurance of an effective *capital loss* in real purchasing power terms.

As to the comparison of bonds to the utility stock portfolio, in terms of capital, historical data in Table 5 shows the following: during each and every decade, the market value of the utility common stocks rose significantly. The amount of increase ranged from 44 to 155 percent with a mean appreciation of 90 percent. Even after eliminating the effect of changes in the price/earnings ratio, which did rise during this postwar period, the appreciation would have ranged from 36

TABLE 5

Capital appreciation of Moody's utilities

Period	Original investment	Tenth year value	Appreciation
1945–54 ....$26.29		$ 44.30	69%
1946–55 .... 34.05		49.24	45
1947–56 .... 29.53		49.62	68
1948–57 .... 27.34		49.42	44
1949–58 .... 28.37		57.96	100
1950–59 .... 31.23		66.35	112
1951–60 .... 32.55		69.82	115
1952–61 .... 35.48		90.55	155
1953–62 .... 37.80		91.50	142
1954–63 .... 44.30		102.79	133
1955–64 .... 49.24		108.76	121
1956–65 .... 49.62		117.08	136
1957–66 .... 49.42		102.90	108
1958–67 .... 57.96		101.87	76
1959–68 .... 66.35		98.37	48
1960–69 .... 69.82		94.55	36
Average appreciation 90%			

to 77 percent due solely to earnings increases. Not surprisingly, the utility equity portfolio produces an important capital advantage over bonds. The magnitude of this advantage is impressive. Using the earlier expectation for utilities of 6 percent growth in earnings, and assuming no change in the price/earnings ratio, the capital invested in utility stocks would increase over a century (if we can contemplate such a long time period) to an amount 256 times its present size!

When long-term corporate bonds reached historically high interest rates during 1970, many latent bond buyers argued quite vigorously that if institutional investors could get 8 and 9 percent contractual yields on bonds of satisfactory quality, then surely bonds were attractive. They usually cited the Lorie & Fisher study of long-term returns on common stocks to show that bond buyers could get competitive returns with less risk. The proposition was certainly appealing, but hardly persuasive. To make their case, these bond advocates were comparing *future* returns in bonds with *past* returns in equities. This false logic does not give recognition to the major declines in prices in *both* capital markets and the probability that if the bond market were to recover, so too would the equity market. The only way that bond proponents could legitimately claim that the historical evidence in favor of stocks was not still valid would be to show somehow that the basic and time-tested relationship between the equity and bond markets had been drastically changed. They have not made this case. There is no evidence that such a case can be made, and subsequent market action in 1971 has once again refuted it.

The remarkable result of our historical analysis is that a portfolio of conservative equities has been and is very likely to continue to be greatly superior to a bond portfolio on all counts:

1) Capital is safer from inflation in equities than in bonds.
2) Equities produce much higher income.
3) Equity income is more predictable.
4) Equities increase capital substantially.

The evidence is impressively in favor of an investment in conservative equities as the preferred means by which a long-term investment portfolio can achieve its goals. Yet, the question remains: Why do most pension funds, endowment funds, and other large, long-term portfolios continue to commit a large percentage of portfolio capital to long-term investments in bonds? The explanation lies partly in the experience fiduciaries have had with terminal estate planning and partly in the difficulty all investment managers face when asked to deal astutely with long time periods. (For many investors five years into the future is really a working definition of infinity.) For an investment manager faced with a heavy volume of daily business demanding immediate decisions, the really long term is a most awesome challenge to the imagination. Thus, the real problem is perhaps not whether bonds are a better source of income and capital values over the longer term, but rather how can and should the investment manager —and his clients—shift to a strange and unfamiliar time dimension—embracing 10, 20, or even 100 years—in which truly relevant long-term policy can be formulated.

If it were decided to change away from a policy of holding a large permanent portfolio of bonds towards a portfolio of conservative common stocks, how should the change in policy be implemented? At least three choices are available: (1) the change can be made in a single, rapidly executed, "do it now" program at a specific time when conditions are deemed propitious; (2) straight bonds can be replaced by convertible issues which will be subsequently converted into common stocks; or (3) a program of dollar averaging can be used to make the transition from bonds to stocks over a period of years. The choice depends in part on the decision makers' confidence in their ability to time the transition from bonds to equities; in part on their confidence that the policy change is soundly conceived; and in part on their appraisal of the risk that if near-term market developments go against the long-term trend and expectation, a sound long-term policy decision might be interrupted or reversed for essentially short-term reasons. In almost any situation, depending on the politics of policy formulation, a sound means can be chosen to achieve the end result of a policy of holding bonds only as needed for permanent defensive reserves. We turn now to other aspects of portfolio policy after which we shall consider portfolio strategy and selection.

4

Policy in portfolio management: Cash

I T IS OBVIOUS that the stock market fluctuates—sometimes by large amounts—so the possibility of selling stocks when the market is high and buying them back when the market is low is intriguing. The opportunity to shift back and forth between stocks and cash and thereby to increase the profitability of the portfolio holds great interest for aggressive portfolio managers. What a mark of distinction it would be to have sold out in the summer of 1929 or the early winter of 1962 or the spring of 1969—*if* the cash were reinvested before the subsequent market recovery. Unfortunately, it has not been possible for any large institutional portfolio manager to come even close to such an achievement. One piece of evidence suggests that market forecasts that lead to increasing and decreasing cash holdings are really just self-fulfilling prophecies: as institutions increase cash positions to defend against an expected market decline, they sell stocks heavily and, apparently, *as a result of their own selling*, the market drops. And then as more positive expectations for the market lead to spending the hoarded cash on stock repurchases, this new buying pressure makes the market rise—just as expected.

Exhibit 1 compares mutual fund cash balances with the S&P market average, showing that they appear to be "reciprocating changes," or that increasing and reducing their cash positions are causing the market averages to fall or rise in approximately direct proportions. In other words, shifting from stocks to cash and then back to stocks by "herds" of institutions is causing the very market swings these "sophisticated" changes in cash reserves are expected to exploit. That

EXHIBIT 1

Fund liquidity

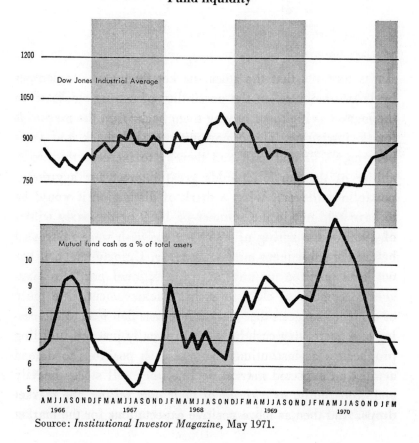

Source: *Institutional Investor Magazine*, May 1971.

would be as impossible as trying to run away from your own shadow! In other words, these funds may well be involved in a game which is at best zero-sum and is quite probably a sure loss for most participants.

But the sheer magnitude of dollars involved—$5 billion from mutual funds alone—necessitates serious consideration. Cash in portfolio policy can be discussed most clearly using the terminology Lord Keynes used in his *General Theory*. That is, the motives for holding cash are three: balances required efficiently to effect normal *operating transactions,* balances that reflect a *precautionary* disposition, and balances that are frankly *speculative.* Keynes discussed cash as an alternative to long-term bonds, but the concepts are perhaps even more appropriate to choices between cash and equities within a large portfolio. Cash balances required for the efficient operation of large portfolios typically run between 2 and 3 percent of the total fund. These *transaction* balances will be used in two ways. First, the portfolio manager may have instructed his trader to buy 100,000 shares of Mattel. This stock usually trades less than 10,000 shares per day, so the trader could perhaps expect to buy 2–3,000 shares each day and gradually build up the desired position. Or he could try to arrange through a "block broker" to buy 30,000 or 50,000 or more shares from another institutional holder. If he can make the purchase in a few quick block transactions, the average price will probably be lower than if he is buying steadily in the auction market every day for two whole months. But to do a block transaction, the trader must have cash on hand. So this is the first reason for having what we call "transaction balances." The second reason for having cash for efficient portfolio operations is that many institutional portfolio managers must be prepared to pay out cash on short notice. This is particularly true of mutual funds which stand ready to redeem shares twice daily "on demand." So they hold some cash as a buffer to insulate portfolio management from the in and out flows of money which are due to client needs that are *quite separate from investment management of the portfolio.*

Using Keynes' terms once again, a slight increase in cash balances, to perhaps 5 to 10 percent, represents an extra cash increment for *precautionary* reasons which may reflect the possibility of a sudden cash withdrawal (perhaps from worried individuals who are mutual fund investors), but more typically reflects the portfolio manager's own cautious views. For example, he may believe the prices of the specific stocks he is buying or selling are "weak" and so will hold back on purchases and accelerate sales—which will result in a moderate increase in the cash position. Increases in cash balances to this precautionary level are primarily a function of the operating situation of a particular portfolio and are not directly related to a general appraisal of the equity market as a whole.

Such is not the case with what can properly be called *speculative* cash balances. These are intentional rather than incidental balances. And they can be quite large. In a survey of a wide range of institutional investors conducted by the author, institutional cash balances were found to range as high as 60 percent of the total portfolio. And the average maximum cash position among these institutions was 30 percent. Since the average size of the portfolios involved was just under $300 million, we are obviously talking about very large amounts of cash being held as "speculative" balances. When portfolio managers raise such large cash balances, their objective is to make a large profit by leaving the stock market when prices are generally high and later returning to the market after a large decline in the general market levels. These "speculative" balances represent an aggressive effort to exploit an expected *opportunity* rather than a defensive effort to minimize or avoid a possible *problem,* as is the case

with precautionary cash balances. These are obviously speculative balances because such cash holdings are a direct win-
lose wager against the equity market as a whole, and even
against the manager's own portfolio.

The evidence in Exhibit 1 demonstrates that such speculative cash balances are an important part of contemporary
portfolio management. Our survey of institutional investors'
practices in respect of cash management shows that mutual
funds and other institutions follow very similar practices in
managing their portfolio cash positions. The aggregate speculative balances of just the mutual funds have ranged above
$5 billion. This is indeed a large sum of money. It is larger
than the money invested by these funds in any single stock,
so at times cash is the largest single investment of the mutual
funds. The total "speculative" balances among all institutional investors including pension funds, endowments, insurance companies, counsellors, and trust companies is, according to the survey mentioned above, several times as large as
those of the mutual funds shown in the chart. This suggests
the possibility that speculative cash balances may at times be
as large as $15 billion.

Such a sum of money represents such an important portfolio management policy practice as to warrant very careful
consideration. The key question is this: are these speculative
cash balances profitable? That is, do portfolio managers improve upon the profits they might have earned by remaining
fully invested? Again our survey of institutional investors
indicates that they believe this cash management exercise to
be generally unprofitable, particularly relative to other activities in which a fund manager might engage—such as being in the best stocks!

The basic argument against switching out of equities and
into cash is given in the long-term rates of return earned in
equities as shown in the Lorie & Fisher study (Table 1). If

the long-term average trend is so profitable, why fool around trying to catch a few "extra" profits? Of course, the answer is that *if* it can be done, the professional portfolio manager should make the necessary effort. So the crux of the problem is this: *can* it be done? In the survey, none of the institutional investors could recall any specific portfolio manager who had been consistently good at calling the market.

The institutional investor who raises a large "speculative" cash balance can increase his portfolio's profit only if he buys back the stocks he sold at lower prices than he originally sold them for. (Of course, he will quite probably buy back somewhat different stocks, but for ease of explanation here we can ignore this minor complicating factor.) In the survey, the portfolio managers were asked about two very different problems: first, by how much do they "miss" the market peaks and bottoms in changing their cash positions?; and second, how much does it "cost" to buy or sell a stock in a $300 million fund? (This "cost" is not just the brokerage commissions, but also includes the more important costs of bidding up the price of a stock while buying it and the cost of accepting a price discount when selling.) Those experienced investors included in the survey believe that the total transaction cost of buying and later selling (or selling and later repurchasing) a normal position in a stock will usually be just under 10 percent. In other words, they report that it costs $4.65 to buy a $100 stock and $5.30 to sell it for a total "round trip" cost of $9.95. The point is that to break even on such a trade (sell the stock to raise cash and then buy the stock back), the portfolio manager must be able to buy the stock back at least 10 percent lower in price.

At first this sounds awfully easy, but another "cost" must also be absorbed before a profit can be made. The investors in the survey reported that they miss the precise turns in the market—some act too early and some act too late—and that on average they miss market tops by 11 percent and miss market bottoms by 10 percent for a combined "error cost" of 21 percent for a typical "round trip." Adding the two costs together, we get a 31 percent "break-even" hurdle rate. That is, institutional portfolio managers say they need to have a 31 percent average change in stock prices to "get out and get back in" without losing money. And that is indeed a rare opportunity. Too rare. During the past 50 years, market swings from peak to trough of 31 percent have occurred only three times—and all before World War II.

It is very difficult to believe that the stock market is not predictable, and that institutional investors cannot find a way to "beat the market." Indeed in recent years, some very interesting work has been done in an effort to analyze and forecast the supply and demand for equities with the thought that if supply and demand for equities could be studied in detail, some useful forecasts of the direction of overall equity prices could then be made. The concept is similar to attempts to analyze and project supply and demand for credit using the Federal Reserve Board's "flow of funds" data and format. Unfortunately, it has thus far been very difficult to make reliable projections of either supply or demand, particularly when long-term projections are required. Consequently, the studies have tended to follow rather than lead the market. For example, during the latter stages of the 1967–68 bull market, several bold studies were published showing how the apparently insatiable appetites of institutional investors would so persistently exceed the supply of new corporate stock issues that the bull market would continue indefinitely. The forecasts were later proven to be too optimistic. Then, after the 1969–70 bear market, other analysts presented studies purporting to show that stock prices could not and would not soon recover. As they say in France, "Plus ça change, plus c'est la même chose." Stocks recovered.

The long-term upward trend of the equity market has several important implications for portfolio policy formulation. First, if the long-run trend is generally in favor of a rising level of stock prices, short-term policy swings in and out of cash are clearly *speculative* maneuvers incurring a high risk of being wrong because the fund manager is working "against the tide." Second, portfolio managers who *insist* on changing their cash/equities ratio should concentrate on going against the crowd, raising their cash when other institutions are reducing cash balances, and cutting back their cash balances when other institutions are building up cash.

Logically (and aesthetically) any fund manager who is willing to hold less than 100 percent in equities, say 80 percent in equities when he is convinced that temporary market conditions are adverse, should be willing to go just as far the other way and *borrow* in order to reach say a 120 percent invested position when the market seems comparably positive. Of course, few if any institutional investors would be willing to "speculate with borrowed money." But then, why will they speculate with their own capital? Perhaps by looking at the "percent in equities" question in this different way, the reader will find the theme of this chapter clearer: institutional investors should not speculate with cash.

Two "other-than-for-profit" reasons are sometimes given for selling stocks to accumulate cash. One is that having 10 to 20 percent of the total fund in cash allows the portfolio manager to live with the ugly strains of having his long-term commitments plummet to lower and lower prices during an adverse market swing. In other words, he will be able to hang on to most of his holdings during the rough period so long as he knows he has a "cache of cash" in reserve. Yet it is apparent that 20 percent is a small part of the total portfolio. So a 20 percent cash reserve is probably at best a palliative and quite probably an illusory haven if the other 80 percent of a portfolio is being drubbed by stock market turbulence. More importantly, a 20 percent cash position too often gives a false sense of security that leads the portfolio manager to hang on to all his old holdings—until the storm is over—when he should really be taking advantage of a strained market to change his stock holdings advantageously, putting his fund in a stronger, more virile position for the future. In investing, as in so many other fields, a strong offense is truly the best defense.

The other nonprofit reasons advanced for having cash is the feeling that "there's nothing really worth buying." This is understandable nonsense. There may be no *new* opportunities that appear worthy of a major commitment and some old holdings may have matured to sale prices. Cash could be the result if there really were no existing holdings that warranted increased investment. Yet, at least *some* of the present holdings in a portfolio of 50 to 70 stocks are worthy of larger dollar investments. And the fund manager who bothers to look for buys in a bear market is usually well rewarded with very profitable opportunities that others are ignoring. In all too many cases, cash offers the investment manager a sterile option to escape from the rigor and anxiety of making stock decisions when the market is strained or in disarray. But since he cannot reasonably expect to "make money with money," this is a false haven.

Despite the logic that argues against shifting between cash and stocks, it is not altogether surprising that increasing and reducing cash positions is a common practice among portfolio managers: it is highly abstract, seductive, and comfortable. It also has the intrigue of being truly "high finance." Unfortunately, it is not profitable. So the profit-maximizing cash policy appears to be to stay fully invested at all times and then make the best of bad markets when they come.

5

Policy in portfolio management: Equities

IF THE first dimension of policy in portfolio management is which market to invest in—bonds, cash, or stocks—the second dimension of policy is what part of the selected market is most attractive. For example, within the bond market there are two well-known policy options: first, How long should bond maturities be? and second, What grade or quality of bond should be held at a particular time in light of present versus historical yields or "yield spreads" between the various categories of bonds? Similar options are available in the equity market, and this aspect of policy in portfolio management is our concern in this chapter.

One of the most important policy issues in the management of large and long-term equity portfolios is the choice of the appropriate "risk class" in which to position the fund, and whether to remain consistently in one "risk class" or to attempt to shift from class to class in response to changing conditions in the market.

In discussing "risk class," we adopt the view that stocks

can be classified or grouped according to their price fluctuation or price "volatility" over relatively short periods of time. However, we do not accept the overbroad generalization that "risk class" represents true risk any more than all quadrupeds are horses, or mules, or jackasses. (Discussion of true risk is reserved for Chapter 13.)

When the market rises, "volatile" stocks over a relatively short period of time rise more rapidly and by greater amounts than the market averages, while less volatile stocks go up by less than the averages. Of course, the reverse is also true: when the overall market declines, prices of volatile stocks go down faster and farther than the less volatile stocks. In general, highly volatile stocks behave as they do because they have any or all of the following characteristics: high rate of current earnings growth, low profit margins, brief or erratic past earnings records, high P/E ratios, highly dynamic business operations, aggressive management, important but uncertain technological developments, etcetera, etcetera. In other words, the *future value* of these stocks is very uncertain, so their *current prices* tend naturally to react swiftly and significantly to changing expectations. That is why they are volatile or "risky" stocks.

In a general sense, the volatility of stocks is caused by investors from time to time substituting caution for confidence (and vice versa). Three aspects of valuation can and do change simultaneously. For example, here is what happens to cause a price to drop. First, the rate at which the future earnings stream is being capitalized declines. Investors decide that the expected earnings in the future, given the risk that expectations may not be realized, is just not worth as much today as it seemed to be worth yesterday. Second, the normal discount for uncertainty about the real shape and trend of the growth of that earnings stream increases. Investors become more conservative in their estimates of potential and probable earnings. And third, the time horizon over which investment appraisals are made becomes much shorter. Investors insist on paying only for the sure and the nearly sure earnings of the next year or two and will not pay for less sure future potential. For all these reasons, stocks that are not highly predictable will decline, and the less their predictability the greater their decline.

In contrast, as investor confidence returns, the very long term becomes the accepted basis upon which potential earnings are estimated, uncertainty declines to a low level and precautionary discounts are put aside, and the evaluation of equity investments in general becomes expansive and generous. These accordian-like elongations and foreshortenings are primarily caused by emotion and are seldom very long lasting. But the swings—both up and down—can be very great. Take for example the price behavior of the common shares of Mohawk Data Sciences:

1966: $19–$4	1969: $89–$60
1967: $99–$6	1970: $87–$18
1968: $111–$54	1971: $47–$22

Since some stocks go up and down by more than other stocks, the portfolio manager might well attempt to exploit differences in price volatility. When markets are high, volatile stocks would have risen more than the general market, and so they could be sold and less volatile stocks bought with the hope of going down by less than the averages in a subsequent market decline. (The process would be reversed after the general market had declined and highly volatile stocks had declined a great deal more, with the more volatile stocks being bought for the faster and longer ride back up.) This practice, like stepping away from equities and into cash or bonds and then moving back into equities again, requires being "right twice." The fund manager must be able to call

risks. In other words, high turnover causes rushed research which causes nervous fund management which leads directly to higher turnover, and the high-volume-low-quality cycle is closed. And the portfolio manager is left in the untenable position of attempting to achieve superior long-run portfolio profits by guessing quickly about prices rather than carefully evaluating values. The tradeoff between investment decision quantity and decision quality should be made with care. Turnover can and should be planned, not left to chance, because turnover is an important factor in organizing the internal and external sources of investment analysis that the fund manager will need.

Stock market reality involves many aspects of liquidity and illiquidity in portfolio operations. If it costs 10 percent to buy and 10 percent to sell, and if the long term of average profit in equities is 10 percent annually, then a 50 percent rate of turnover would *ceteris paribus* fully cancel out the profit trend and leave the investor with zero growth. This warrants some thought. There is a surprising tendency for investors to make decisions on distressingly small differences in price, which is why the English maxim about being penny wise but pound foolish has real meaning in the management of large equity portfolios. For example, the portfolio manager who intends to sell a very large position in a relatively illiquid stock will often refuse a bid that is only slightly below his initial offering price. He does not seem to realize that the bid that seems low is probably above the average price at which the shares will actually be sold because even if his "target price" is where the selling program begins, as the selling continues the price will probably sag lower. Most portfolio managers should test themselves on this by conscientiously estimating the average price at which their fund will buy or sell each stock and comparing their estimates with the actual results. They would probably be surprised. Again, our survey respondents estimate the cost of a "round trip" at 10 percent. One large institution studied its own record carefully and found the cost even higher.

The essential message of this chapter is quite simple: diversification is important to large portfolios of volatile stocks chosen as a class; concentration is important when stocks are selected individually; and high turnover is very expensive both in undermining decision quality and in the full cost of transactions.

8

Portfolio analysis

A WELL-DESIGNED PORTFOLIO is worth more than the sum of its stocks. Yet little attention has been paid in the past to describing how large, diversified equity portfolios, as composite entities, can and do have characteristics that differ significantly from the characteristics of the component stocks. (The brief summary in Chapter 7 of Markowitz' thinking about building superior portfolios from inferior stocks was an early effort in this direction.) Sound portfolio descriptions can provide important insight and guidance to the portfolio manager. Since a well-constructed portfolio is far more than a list of stocks—the whole is both greater than and different from the sum of its parts—the purpose of portfolio analysis is to provide clear statements about the investment characteristics of the portfolio as a whole. Such descriptive statements can be made for a particular *point* in time or for any desired *period* of time. That is, descriptive statements can be made about a fund either statically or dynamically. First the ways in which a portfolio can be described as of a particular point in time will be explored, then the dynamic descriptions will be covered. (Of course, comparing several sequential static descriptions of a portfolio will give some valuable insight into its dynamic characteristics.)

The most common static description is simply an inventory listing of the stocks held. Although such lists can be made quite useful to the portfolio manager, the conventional practice of breaking the list down into standard industry groupings is—due to the increasing complexity of American business—usually more harm than help. Are General Motors and American Motors really similar companies? Is Occidental Petroleum more like Gulf Oil, Allied Chemical, or Gulf & Western? Is Sperry Rand an "electronics" company or an "office equipment" company or neither? Rather than force these procrustean standard groups upon the stocks in a portfolio, a more useful purpose would be served by presenting the portfolio in terms of the groups that the fund manager thinks of when he develops portfolio strategy. Thus, for example, a strategic play in housing might include Skyline Homes (a mobil home builder), Armstrong (carpets, ceilings, and furnishings), Whirlpool (home appliances), Boise Cascade (building materials and residential developments), and First Charter Financial (savings and loans). Two points: not every stock has to be jammed into a group; some stocks will be held without a group concept. And some stocks will show up in more than one group—First Charter might also be part of an "interest rate" group.

Dividing the total portfolio into a few major stock categories is helpful when the fund follows an investing philosophy that is based on using only a few basic types of stocks. For example, one institution groups stocks into "high growth," "moderate-steady growth," "cyclical growth," and "other" on its portfolio statements. Another uses "technology," "business services," "consumer services," and "financial" groupings. Percentages are shown for these broad categories and for the individual stocks in the list. This is important because the portfolio should be managed in terms of the total size of each holding and its percentage weight in the fund; share prices, number of shares held, tax costs, and the like are not very important when thinking about the portfolio as a portfolio and should not be given the attention so commonly accorded them. (Perhaps they should be carried on a supplemental page.)

The basic portfolio listing by stock "type" with dollar size of holding and percentages for each type and holding should be prepared daily. It should include price changes for each stock during the last day, week, and month to help the manager recognize the price activity of the stock. The strategy groupings—including both stocks held and stocks contemplated for purchase—should also be prepared frequently, and preferably daily. These are the immediate action reports; others involve equally important, but less critical decisions.

Reports on the portfolio that might be made weekly, quarterly, or monthly and that can help the manager make more effective decisions about the market factors in his portfolio over the long run include the following: division of holdings among stocks listed on the New York Stock Exchange, those listed on the American Stock Exchange, and those traded over the counter; various measures of portfolio concentration such as the number of stocks held, the average size in dollars, the percentage of the fund invested in the 5 largest, 10 largest, and 20 largest individual holdings; the stocks held in the portfolio which are experiencing unusually high levels of trading activity relative to their past norms or relative to their total number of outstanding shares; the stocks for which the number of shares held exceeds ten days of trading volume in the current market; and the stocks in which mutual funds together hold 10 percent and 20 percent of the total shares.

Other ways of analyzing the portfolio in "fundamental"

terms that can be useful are these: What is the average P/E of the portfolio and how does this differ by decile? What is the five-year average past earnings per share for each P/E decile? What year-to-year gain in earnings is expected this year for each P/E decile?

Another portfolio characteristic that can be analyzed usefully is the price volatility of the portfolio as a whole, or by segment, and how volitility has changed over time. It is possible for a portfolio to shift significantly away from its long-term policy in an unintended way, and careful tracking of the portfolio's relative volatility can help the fund manager hold to a steady course. To carry the nautical analogy further, the portfolio manager might well shift his funds' relative volatility so that it moves against the tide of the general market. In this way, volatility is the highest at market bottoms (in anticipation of a recovery) and lowest at market highs (to protect against a decline). The straight course is sailed by adjusting to the currents and tides of the market.

Much of the value of these reports will come from comparing them from one to another and over several periods to see what kinds of changes most help the portfolio and what kinds of changes are either unintentional or harmful. The serious portfolio manager can learn much by studying his fund and himself during various business and stockmarket cycles.

Changes in the holdings of the portfolio can and should be studied at regular intervals. For example, on at least a quarterly basis the fund manager should consider these questions: How have the top five and top ten individual stock holdings changed? Since these major holdings are usually the ones in which the manager has the most conviction, if he is selling them because the "fundamentals" of value are deteriorating too frequently, he has a vastly different portfolio management problem than he would have if the prices had risen so much that he had been "forced" to make a profitable sale.

How much more or less profitable in percentage terms have the major holdings been relative to the rest of the portfolio during the past week, month, quarter, and year? Is concentration helping or hurting the fund? Are the large holdings different in volatility, yield, P/E, growth rate, etc. than the other holdings in the fund? If so, what do such differences imply? What should the manager do?

Since the cost of buying and selling very large positions will be even greater than our survey's 10 percent average, turnover in the major holdings is particularly costly. The portfolio manager should have a more refined way of analyzing turnover than the simple $\frac{\text{Buys} + \text{Sells}}{2} = \text{Turnover}$. Turnover for the 5 and 10 and 20 largest holdings should be calculated separately because it means something quite different. In addition, fund turnover should be measured not only in terms of the average holding period of the average stock but also by the number of stocks and their dollar value held for 3 months and less, 3 to 6 months, 6 to 9 months, 9 to 12 months, 12 to 18 months, 18 to 24 months, and over 2 years. Two funds may both have an average turnover of 80 percent and yet be very different. One may be very active in the three-month period and then hold for the long term most of the stocks that survive a "trial marriage," while the other fund may bunch most of its activity around the six-to-nine-month period. Again, studying changes in the turnover pattern of the individual fund, particularly relative to the market cycle, can be particularly useful. Stock portfolios should have a pattern of "spaced maturities" just as bond portfolios often have. A portfolio is stronger if its holdings have different life cycles and expected payoff periods. (Perhaps the greatest weakness of the "go-go" funds is their unnatural scramble to own only those stocks in a "profits now" phase. Skimming the profits cream off the *S* curve of a stock's maturity cycle is really impossible in a large fund and all too frequently means missing the really outstanding profit opportunities that require a longer investment maturity cycle.)

Again on a regular basis, the portfolio manager should compare his sales with his purchases during past periods to see whether the new stocks outperformed the old; and if so, why; and if not, why not? He may be able to identify regular patterns of strength and/or weakness in his decision making. For example, one portfolio manager found that he usually lost relative performance when he bought stocks with P/E multiples between 12 and 24 times estimated earnings even though both the lower and higher multiple stocks worked well for him. He does not buy middle multiple stocks anymore.

Many other portfolio characteristics can be profitably analyzed to determine the nature of the aggregate fund. One useful procedure is to analyze the fund's holdings of various industry groups in comparison to the industrial weightings of a stratified sample of the total equity market. Usually the subject fund is compared to the Standard & Poor's 500 Stock Index because this index has been carefully constructed to represent a stratified sample of the total equity market and is easily divided into industry segments. (See Table 6.) The assumption of such a comparison is that the portfolio manager is trying to beat the S&P Index and, after studying this hypothetical competitor's "bets," simply decides which industries he will bet on more heavily and which he will bet on less than the market as represented by the S&P 500. If the portfolio manager is "neutral" about a particular industry group, he simply matches the S&P "bet." He would invest *no* money in a group *only* if he were convinced a substantial *negative* bet is proper. This approach to portfolio analysis—betting against all the "house" bets—can provide a useful discipline for the manager and also help him keep his investment horizons as wide as possible. Of course, it is possible to use the

TABLE 6

**Portfolio of actual versus Standard & Poor's
500 Stock Index**

	Actual	*S&P*	*Variance*
Raw materials	12.1%	14.8%	(2.7)%
Oils	12.1	14.5	(2.4)
Intermediate products	7.9	18.3	(10.4)
Building materials	1.9	0.8	1.1
Chemicals	6.0	9.6	(2.4)
Tire and rubber	—	1.0	(1.0)
Capital goods	30.4	23.1	7.3
Aerospace	3.8	1.9	1.9
Agricultural equipment	1.3	0.5	0.8
Business equipment	10.7	9.0	1.7
Construction equipment ...	2.1	0.7	1.4
Electrical equipment	8.1	6.3	1.8
Electronics	3.4	1.2	2.2
Machinery	1.0	0.7	0.3
Railroad equipment	—	0.2	(0.2)
Consumer durables	3.9	8.1	(4.2)
Autos	3.9	6.8	(2.9)
Appliances	0	1.1	(1.1)
Consumer nondurables	20.9	17.2	3.7
Drugs	10.3	3.2	7.1
Food	4.8	5.8	(1.0)
Personal care	2.0	1.4	(0.6)
Photography	2.0	0.7	1.3
Retail-general	1.8	3.7	(1.9)
Noncyclical services	24.5	14.9	9.6
Banks	8.1	—	(8.1)
Insurance	2.3	—	2.3
Utilities	14.1	5.6	8.5

simple strategy of just changing one of the S&P weightings
and counting on that one change to "beat" the S&P, but the
sensible fund manager will spread his bets and make a diversified group of both pro and con decisions. The real advantage of this method of portfolio analysis is that it is dynamic; as the market shifts over time, the so-called house

bets change accordingly. This in turn requires the portfolio manager to respond dynamically. A major risk in portfolio management is standing still and letting external change wear away the strength of the fund's former strategy.

The use of the S&P Index in dynamic portfolio analysis allows the portfolio analyst to study several aspects of portfolio management virtually simultaneously. First, the stocks in the S&P Index are divided into broad categories of business activity so the portfolio analyst can determine whether the portfolio has correctly given above average emphasis to those groups that have outperformed the broad Index or whether the profitability of the fund, relative to the profitability of the Index, has been held back by having too much capital committed to underperforming areas. In other words, strategy can easily be studied. The second aspect of analysis is concerned with the specific selections in a single category to determine whether the selections have improved or restrained the relative profitability of the category-by-category deployment of the portfolio's capital. For example, in Exhibit 3, for three consecutive quarters the portfolio analyzed here has benefited because the S&P 500 rose in value; the capital goods sector rose more than the S&P 500 and the specific capital goods stocks in the portfolio outperformed the S&P sector.

This kind of analysis can also give the portfolio manager useful insights into his own organization's strengths and weaknesses in investment selection. In addition, this method of analysis can help instill a keen sense of competition within an entire investment organization because it is competing against a known adversary and can try to beat him at any and all levels. (It also can help clients understand what is involved in the complex business of investment management.) There are on the other hand two problems with this form of portfolio analysis: the analysis is all retrospective rather than

EXHIBIT 3

Performance analysis—capital goods sector

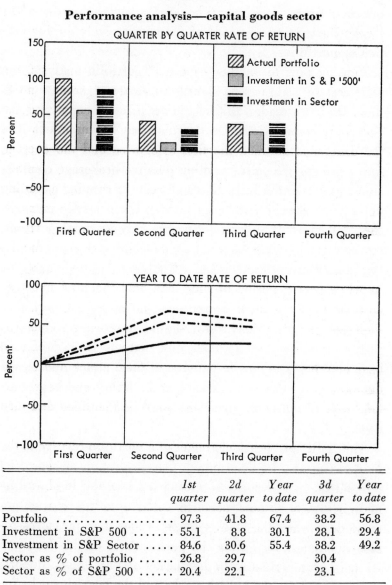

	1st quarter	2d quarter	Year to date	3d quarter	Year to date
Portfolio	97.3	41.8	67.4	38.2	56.8
Investment in S&P 500	55.1	8.8	30.1	28.1	29.4
Investment in S&P Sector	84.6	30.6	55.4	38.2	49.2
Sector as % of portfolio	26.8	29.7		30.4	
Sector as % of S&P 500	20.4	22.1		23.1	

Note: All rates of return are on an annual basis, compounded quarterly.

Source: Donaldson, Lufkin & Jenrette, Inc.

forward looking—the future is the only place where profits can be made—and it puts too much emphasis on "beating" the S&P Index, which may be an inadequate portfolio objective during some periods of the market cycle, or for particular portfolios.

Turning now to another aspect of portfolio analysis, the *total* cost of transactions should be reviewed from time to time. On block trades, this cost is the price discount plus the brokerage commissions. On "regular way" transactions it is the difference between the first sale price and the average sale price for the entire position plus the brokerage commissions. (Perhaps the fully allocated costs of running a trading department should also be included.) The portfolio manager should then analyze the relationship between total portfolio return, transaction costs, and gain or loss due to changing the composition of the portfolio. This analysis, repeated at regular intervals over a period of time, can help the fund manager determine the optimum degree of turnover for his portfolio. Past studies have clearly shown that higher turnover enhances profits in strong bull markets and detracts from profits in bear markets. The classic patterns of open attack and closed defense seem to be at work here, so both bull and bear market levels of optimum turnover should be identified and then used.

The "bull" or "bear" character of a portfolio relative to the market can also be determined. One institution measures its portfolio's defensiveness by measuring how the fund and its main strategic groups perform relative to the market on those days when the market declines and then measures offensive strength by testing the performance of the fund and its main groups relative to the market on "up" days. Reports are prepared for the bullish stocks and the bearish stocks for the past week, month, and quarter. As a result, they know which portions of the fund are bearish or bullish and how greatly they are bearish and bullish.

This analysis of upside/downside price behavior is a way of gaining insight into the problem that was central to Markowitz' studies: Do the stocks in the portfolio move in various different ways or do they all move together in response to the same stimulus? If they all move together, then the portfolio has not been given the special strength it should have. This suggests another useful exercise. Over the past year or so, have the stocks in the portfolio reacted differently or similarly in response to such stimuli as a change in the prime rate, the number of cars sold, housing starts, Vietnam news, wage settlements, inflation, or tax changes? In a well-balanced portfolio, the individual holdings will behave differently. And this means that the actual returns earned in the fund are more reliably earned than would have been the case if the stocks' individual returns had bunched closely together and reacted comparably to each significant stimulus.

Studies of the relative profitability of all individual holdings should be undertaken on a regular, if not a continuous basis, to determine which are outperforming the total fund and which are underperforming. This keeps the portfolio manager's attention always focused on the unusual parts of the portfolio, because this is where major successes and major failures will be found early. Since the most prevalent problem in portfolio management is having too little committed to the most profitable selections and too much committed to the least profitable areas, this analysis of internal relative performance can greatly help the portfolio manager increase the returns in the portfolio by regularly forcing him to reconsider his own decisions and encouraging him to act more boldly with the better decisions.

Finally, the performance of the total portfolio, relative to market averages and relative to other funds of similar size with similar goals should be reviewed regularly. Several firms now provide sophisticated performance measurement services which are worthwhile.

Before concluding this chapter, a few brief notes should be made on the kinds of errors that are frequently made in portfolio operations. The portfolio analyst should look for these common symptoms of portfolio malaise. One is phony diversification in which the portfolio has investments in 60 different stocks, giving the superficial appearance of broad diversification, even though the 10 largest holdings represent a third to one half of total assets, which is really aggressive *non*diversification. Another common problem is that the largest holdings in a fund too often reflect past realized profits rather than expected future profits. A profit-maximizing portfolio should look only to the future and quite vigorously sell the most successful holdings of the past (which are often growing stale) unless they are also expected to be the most successful holdings for the future. Another related problem is allowing the portfolio to accumulate "scraps" or partial positions in stocks not fully sold or only slightly bought. Regular pruning of the portfolio will eliminate deadwood and also the useless, potentially harmful, small branches that can clutter the fund and interfere with the strong growth of the major branches.

Another common problem, which was alluded to above, is allowing price volatility to become higher as the market rises towards a cyclical peak, or conversely to allow price volatility to be at its lowest after a major market decline when a recovery might have a multiplying profit if the portfolio holdings were high in volatility. Actually, if it is going to be managed at all, portfolio price volatility should be minimized when the market price level appears relatively low. The genesis of the error here—as in most other portfolio errors—is structuring the portfolio to meet the past rather than the future.

This chapter has focused on the large equity portfolio as a distinctive entity with its own character. Each of the specific techniques discussed here can be used to gain insight into and understanding of the internal strengths and weaknesses of a particular portfolio either statically or dynamically. These analytical techniques should be used vigorously in portfolio management because they deal directly with the three primary dimensions of portfolio structure: policy, strategy, and selection. Shifting now from "macroanalysis" to "microanalysis," the next chapter begins a series on analysis of the individual investments that make up the portfolio that we have heretofore considered only as a whole.

9

Opportunity analysis

THIS CHAPTER is the first of a series dealing with five phases of investment analysis: business analysis, financial analysis, market analysis, risk analysis, and opportunity analyis. We begin with opportunity analysis and conclude with risk analysis. And throughout, we maintain a portfolio orientation because the usefulness of each kind of analysis is entirely a function of the contribution it makes to portfolio profitability. The purpose of this chapter on opportunity analysis is to identify the investment characteristics of those stocks that can add significantly to portfolio profit. Unless investors know what they are looking for, how will they recognize significant investment opportunity when they find it?

There is one great way to achieve substantial portfolio profits in individual equities: buy and hold the common shares of outstanding companies which are able to create such enormous and continuing opportunity for their own profitable growth that their year-to-year gains in value so greatly exceed the profit objectives of the portfolio that they can and should be held with only occasional consideration of market price. Great companies determine their own destiny; they control their environment, they create their own growth, they initiate change and manage it. The resources the great company brings to the business arena are so valuable that the potential growth of the company is open-ended; no horizons, limits, or boundaries restrict its potential. The management knows quite definitely what it will try to achieve and how it will proceed, because it has chosen to limit the company's activities to a small minority of the business it *could* engage in to be sure that it only attempts those things at which it can excel.

Great companies depend so substantially upon the excellence of their people that it is not possible to overstress this point. They have abundant, even redundant management talents so that present problems can virtually be overwhelmed, while the "excess" managers are vigorously creating new opportunities for the company to pursue. Great companies always have clear, strong, and timely operating control over their businesses. Great companies are always—without any exceptions whatsoever—great marketing companies that create lasting, lusting customers because they themselves create goods and services of extraordinary value to these customers. Of course, great companies make for great stocks, stocks which will rise through many different market phases and which can and should be held for very long periods (Coca Cola, Avon, Xerox, IBM, and Polaroid, are all examples). Unfortunately, these great companies are few. Still, investors must understand the investment nature of great companies or they may fail to realize what they are *not* getting in their usual investments.

Although we must concern ourselves primarily with the investment opportunities provided by more ordinary companies, the importance of understanding what opportunity is and where to find it is still very great. The primary purpose of opportunity analysis is to identify substantial discrepancies between value and price where value is the true worth of a security when fairly appraised in terms of its long-term prospects, and price is the current, perhaps temporary balance between today's demand and today's supply. Since, over very long periods of time, the price of an equity will fluctuate around, but also tend to approximate the long-term value of that equity, the investment decision maker who both understands long-term values and appreciates the behavior of near-term prices can make substantial profits by capitalizing upon the differences. Obviously, he would try to buy when value exceeds price or sell when price exceeds value. But also, he can look through the current behavior of prices and select for major emphasis in the portfolio those securities or groups of securities which have the most rapidly rising values. (One of the most common errors in selection is to assume that rapidly rising prices mean rapidly rising values.) And, if the portfolio manager elects to retain a stock whose price has exceeded its value, he will be clear in his own mind that he is holding only for price or trading reasons and so will be particularly sensitive to hints of price deterioration. So the real purpose of opportunity analysis is to keep the fund manager well informed about the short versus the long term, the trading position versus the investment commitment, and the price versus the value of the securities in his portfolio.

Since opportunity depends primarily on value, we need to be clear on the basis of value. Investment value can arise from only four different sources: earnings, dividends, assets, and hope. In some ways, particularly over the very long term and in the abstract, each of these sources of value is linked to each of the other sources, but it is very unusual for more than one source of value to influence price significantly at any one time. And it is extremely rare for the price-determining source of value to change from one of these four to any other, particularly in the short run. Of course earnings, particularly growing earnings, will lead to higher dividend payments and to rising accumulation of assets, but the valuation of these same shares in terms of per share assets or dividend yields will always be less than the valuation based upon the conviction that earnings will continue to grow at a high and sustained rate. For example, IBM's earnings may be worth $300 per share, while its dividend alone would support a price of only $100 per share and its net assets would be "worth" only $60 per share. Of course, IBM sells at over $300, so in appraising the worth of a growth stock, the only importance of assets and dividends is their ability to add to or detract from future growth in earnings because earnings determine investment value.

This important proposition may be emphasized with an example showing why DuPont's common shares were so obviously a sale at nearly $300 per share in 1964. The DuPont Company followed the practice of investing only in projects that returned 20 percent on capital invested *before* allowing for depreciation. In addition, a long-standing policy called for paying out as dividends approximately 70 percent of earnings each year. Since the company had only moderate excess cash and was unwilling to use substantial debt financing, its maximum long-term growth rate was only 6 percent, assuming they achieved 20 percent returns on the 30 percent of earnings retained for reinvestment each year. The only way DuPont could escape this slow growth rut would be to get higher than 20 percent returns on new investments or change its arcane financial policies. Because of an unhappy experience with some Philadelphia bankers in the mid-19th century, DuPont management abhored and eschewed debt of any kind four generations later. Unfortunately, business analysis clearly demonstrated that the company was not reaching the 20 percent profit goal on new projects. Even more serious, on investments made in previous years, past rates of return which had often been very high were steadily deteriorating. Consequently, not only was DuPont limiting its potential growth to 6 percent per annum, but also its past successes were fading and threatened to result in a noticeable shortfall below this modest ceiling. In fact, during the next five years, per share earnings actually declined and the shares fell 69 percent in price to $92 before the end of the decade! Even though assets accumulated and dividends were increased, since the common stock was priced and valued in terms of earnings growth, a failure to realize upon either potential or expectations led directly to a major decline in both value and price.

An example of mixing up the sources of investment value occurs from time to time in metal stocks, particularly Anaconda. Most of the metal producers' stocks are held for their dividends by investors seeking a high current yield on their investment. They are not valued on per share earnings, and rising earnings will not increase the value of the shares to these yield-oriented shareholders unless these earnings allow the management to pay a higher per share dividend for a sustained period into the future. In the case of Anaconda, a romantic and genuinely exciting company, even though earnings add to value only by way of increasing the dividend, from time to time a two- or three-year progression of higher and higher earnings attracts a group of innocent Wall Streeters who think in terms of earnings growth rates when evaluating equities. They see earnings rising rapidly and hear geologists talk about explorations in the jungles of the world. "Sure," they say, "there are risks, but the stock is selling at only an 8 P/E and per share earnings are going up at a 20 percent compounded rate! Even a P/E of 12 would mean a hefty 50 percent profit. And of course with all that exploration, something wonderful just might happen. Obviously, the stock of this great company is substantially undervalued relative to earnings." So they buy the stock. And for a while the stock rises in price because this new demand for the shares absorbs the available supply and then bids up the price. After a time, however, the rising share price reduces the dividend yield, and the high-yield-seeking stockholders out in Indiana begin to sell their holdings because the price exceeds their dividend yield value. And as their "inadequate yield" supply increases, it overwhelms the "cheap on earnings" demand and the share price drops back towards the original price. This so discourages the earnings-growth-stock-appreciation investors that they also sell. Before long, the only investors willing to hold the shares are the folks out in Indiana who still determine value according to dividends, and are once again interested in Anaconda now that the shares are back at their original prices. Once again, the key to knowing what investment opportunity is *not* is to understand how value is actually being measured.

Hope is a curious source of valuation as demonstrated from time to time by the price behavior of advanced technology company stocks that drop in price just as the company breaks out of the red and starts to earn a profit. Now that the company is earning a profit, there is a price/earnings ratio, and often it is so very high that realism dampens the prior enthusiasm of pure, unadulterated hope.

The last way in which a stock's price can be supported—other than earnings and dividend yield—is the per share assets of the corporation. Asset value stocks like gold mines and land companies can enjoy rising prices *even though earnings are declining* if investors are convinced that the value of their assets is increasing sufficiently. This happens in gold stocks every time there is serious talk of devaluing the dollar. "The mines are losing money, but are full of gold that could be profitably mined at higher prices." While this sort of thing is amusing to watch, it is important as a demonstration of what is and is not investment opportunity in each type of stock.

Each basis of stock valuation is quite different from the others. Asset valuation reflects the past earnings of a company, and the investors attracted to assets seek primarily to conserve capital. Dividend values come from a company's present earnings and attract investors who seek to maximize their current income. Earnings growth valuation depends upon the future of a company's earning power and attracts investors who seek to make their capital productive over long periods of time. The *different* sources of value in common stocks have *different* time horizons and *different* investor constituencies. They seldom mix well. So the essential prerequisite to useful opportunity analysis is to recognize the particular source of value in a stock and the investment objectives of those investors who make the market in that particular stock. Otherwise, the value-to-price relationship may be badly misunderstood and costly errors made in the portfolio.

There is one exception to the rule of consistency in the basis of value for common stocks. Asset valuation can be replaced by earnings growth valuation if substantial changes are made by management so that redundant or underproductive assets are redeployed into more profitable, more vigorous businesses. This change from assets to earnings valuation can greatly change the value of an equity and therefore change the share price considerably. In the early sixties, Chrysler's common stock rose nearly 500 percent in less than four years after George Love of Consolidated Coal and the Rockefellers bought a sufficiently large position to control the company. These potential investment profits are why "turn-around" situations are so popular among investors. And since the companies involved are often quite large, large institutional portfolios are particularly keen on these opportunities. While the continuing vegetation of large corporations with extensive underutilized assets is a major failure of our nation's business economy and one that must be overcome, effecting a successful turnaround is not easy. Far easier to promise than to deliver, most of these situations are disappointing. All too often the projected change is not attained, usually because it was never within the time and cost tolerances of "turnaround" investors.

The thrust of this chapter and the next few chapters can now be summarized in this way. While opportunity analysis can determine whether the profit *potential* is high, financial analysis must be used to determine whether high profits are *possible*, and business analysis must be relied upon to determine whether high profits are *probable*.

In equity investments, the major profits (and the major losses) come from price changes caused by major changes in investor expectations. Since it is far easier to move a company's investment reputation from "very bad" up to "average" than to shift from "average" to "very good" (it is far easier to move a company from badly managed to mediocre in its business operations), most major investment profits come from investors changing their expectations from very low to moderately good. (This is one of the reasons the emphasis in Chapter 5 was put on volatile stocks.) On the other hand, losses occur principally when investors downgrade their expectations for the company in question from very good to only mediocre. In either case, the three Ps—Potential, Possible, and Probable—are useful guides to sound thinking and put proper emphasis upon the importance of effective business analysis, the subject of Chapter 11. In the case of potential profit, business analysis is on the offensive and focuses on improvement opportunities. When confronting potential loss, business analysis is defensive and concentrates on problems that might adversely affect the company or its stock.

Changes in investor expectations for companies and their stocks do not come only from internal developments; external changes can also be important (see Chapter 6). When the business environment changes, the most profitable equity investments are usually made in the best and in the worst companies in the affected group. The reasons behind this best-or-worst thesis are simply that the best company will be able to take substantial extra advantage of a better environmental opportunity, and the worst company will have had such poor prior profitability that any absolute improvement will loom quite large in terms of percentage improvement. For example, if product demand exceeds supply in a particular industry, prices will firm up and the badly run company will no longer resort to price cutting to get orders. Instead it will have fully priced orders for most or all of its capacity, with the result that its current profits will be greatly increased. And the magnitude of percentage increase from the "rising tide" of higher demand will be more for the company that usually has the lowest profit margins in the industry than for the reasonably well-run companies that have been earning reasonably good profits.

The superior company, on the other hand, will not just have higher profits from higher prices, but will also take much greater advantage of the current strength of demand by developing stronger ties with major customers, investing in R&D to develop new products and new processes, developing special product features that will hold customers long after the general demand has abated, or simply demonstrating that it has a superior ability to meet sophisticated customer needs even when volume demand is strong. So there is a solid logic behind the proposition that when the external environment is the cause of improving investor expectations, the best and worst companies offer the greatest investment profit opportunities. This sort of thing happens in the building materials industry in virtually every housing cycle. It also happens in textiles and other semicommodity industries.

Changes in investor expectations are not always caused by *major* changes in company profits or prospects. Sometimes the changes appear rather *minor:* a slowdown or, much more rarely, a speedup in long-run earnings growth. A change in the rate of change is always important because it always changes investment value and because it also causes a change in investor expectations which in turn will change price. Investors become accustomed to a certain characteristic pattern of earnings from each company or common stock, and investors accord that pattern of earnings an approximate valuation per dollar earned in the form of a price/earnings ratio. If the characteristic earnings pattern is changed, the valuation ratio will change, too.

The speed with which investors change that valuation ratio will be primarily a function of the length of time that that characteristic pattern of earnings has been sustained in the past. In other words, the longer a given pattern of earnings has proven "right" for a company and its investors, the longer investors will continue to apply the former valuation ratio after the earnings pattern has changed. Some observers have argued that the stability of the valuation ratio is a function of the aggressiveness of the investors who make the market in the shares, and that conservative investors will hold to an obsolete valuation ratio long after more aggressive investors would have changed. There is another side to this proposition: conservative investors wait until a characteristic earnings pattern and the correlative valuation ratio are well established before investing; they can expect them to hold true for a long period. When they are wrong in their judgments, they take a long time to change their judgments and do so only gradually because they are as cautious in rejecting as they are cautious in accepting a valuation ratio.

Another kind of change in investor expectations deserves mention here because it can involve quite extraordinary profits. This is the change that occurs when increasing numbers of investors and increasing amounts of capital are "introduced" to a new company. They go from expecting literally nothing to expecting a great deal. Prices can appreciate substantially with absolutely no change in the long-term value, provided a significant change occurs in the total demand for that equity. (These sharp changes in share prices can make even venture capital appear profitable.) Of course, sometimes those exuberant valuations are right, sometimes they are wrong. If Xerox is an example of the former, Four Seasons Nursing Homes, which rose 1800 percent in two years and then went bankrupt in the next year, was an example of the latter.

All of the preceding discussion has been based upon changes in companies or groups of companies which were considered by themselves, isolated from the capital market as a market. It would be unrealistic not to recognize the great importance of the market context and the many alternatives that are available in that market. No investment is an island unto itself. Each is part of every other, and their value and price are never absolutes, but are meaningful only relative to each other. So serious discussion of opportunity analysis must be converted to *relative* terms: relative value, relative earnings, and relative price. Even opportunity must be viewed as a relative matter in managing large-equity portfolios. But as was explained in an earlier chapter's discussion of how superior relative earnings can also produce a gain in the relative price earnings multiplier, there is opportunity in these relative forces.

The primary purpose of this chapter on opportunity analysis has been to describe as clearly as possible what kinds of situations can produce substantial portfolio profits. The investment manager must know what he is looking for so he will know what to do with it when he finds it. No investment manager will long achieve portfolio profits in excess of his aspirations; he will not do better than he tries to do. With a clear understanding of the nature of major investment opportunity, he can aim appropriately high and then use financial and business analysis to determine whether the potential is possible and probable.

10

Financial analysis

ALL INVESTORS buy and sell common stocks based upon perceived values that are in turn based almost entirely upon financial descriptions of businesses. And they pay precise prices that are also quoted in dollars. So financial analysis is obviously important, and investors must understand the language of accounting and how it can and will represent changing business realities. However, this chapter focuses primarily on what financial analysis *cannot* do because for most institutional investors the great amount of time, energy, and skill put into financial analysis—and the resulting heavy dependence on "the numbers"—is unwise.

Financial analysis is only quantitative. It deals only with the representation of reality; with the maps, not the actual land and sea; with symbols rather than with the actual business that is symbolized. It accepts the accountant's assumption that all things can be fairly represented in dollar terms. The assumption of universal "dollar equivalency" is false even though it appears to have great precision, accuracy, and validity when the numbers are carried out to the second decimal—even when aggregating billions of dollars in a single entry.

Before discussing the primary—and useful—techniques of financial analysis, it may serve an important purpose to pause briefly to explain why "generally accepted accounting principles" may well be generally *unacceptable* to professional investors. The basic problem with accounting is that accounting reports can be and often are *managed* reports. Management controls the accounting procedures used in reporting results to investors. But management does *not* use these stockholder reports for taxes or for major creditors or even for management's own purposes. Only investors use them. On the other hand, while managers, creditors, and tax assessors specify the data that management must provide to them, investors have no real influence on the form or content of the reports they receive. This situation leads easily to misunderstandings and misrepresentation. More than a few managements have deliberately manipulated their stockholder reports (but always somehow within the broad bounds of generally accepted accounting principles) to make current earnings appear much higher than they might otherwise appear, with the specific purpose being to give investors an overly otimistic appearance of earnings growth. (Virtually all of the "conglomerates" of a few years ago were guilty on this charge.)

Other managers have intentionally held earnings down in fortuitous periods to protect investors from becoming "unduly optimistic" and then padded earnings in poor profit periods to keep investors from becoming "too pessimistic." In some cases, this latter group of managers may well be trying to serve the best long-term interests of the company and its investor-owners, but even with the best intentions, they are manipulating "earnings," and all too often when managers manipulate earnings, they make earnings look better than they are . . . until the result of unsustainable artificial enhancement is an inevitably large disappointment after the ball is over. The financial analyst should be particularly skeptical of "managed earnings" because more and more companies deliberately manipulate their accounting policies to smooth out the ups and downs, particularly the downs, of business profits. When Control Data "sold" some $100 million of computers to its Commercial Credit subsidiary, was this intentionally done to move $16 million of "profits" over to the "high P/E" part of the business? Were they really "earnings"? The GAAP now in use in the United States were designed to prevent promoters from misrepresenting corporate assets and "book values"; they were *not* designed to assure fairness and consistency in the reporting of per share earnings, which is where modern manipulators are most active. The problem this poses for the financial analyst is simple—he can't rely upon the accounting reports for serious investment analysis. Not only is it impossible for him to get a sound understanding of the real business, but even more important, he will never know when profit "reserves" have been completely used up and when no "cushion" is left. A profits shortfall will come as an acute surprise to the many investors who had been counting on the continuing smooth regularity of reported earnings progress. And, of course, by then it is too late; investor expectations will have been shattered, and the stock price will have collapsed. This kind of reaction is what took the common stock of A-T-O, Inc. (formerly Automatic Sprinkler Corporation) from $74 to $20 in a few months during 1968. Many investors accept all too casually the validity of reported earnings, particularly per share earnings: the proverbial "bottom line." Since reported per share earnings have a major impact on both perceived value and price, the financial analyst must recognize that in a very real sense accounting is a game and that even the players who play rough are also within the rules. Generally accepted accounting principles will no more protect investors from large losses than the Marquis of Queensberry's Rules will protect a boxer from being badly beaten.

Another important limitation on the usefulness of financial analysis is that accountants do not include in their reports many of the most important business resources of a company. No audit is made or reported on management skill, imagination, drive, and experience; no entry shows whether management is thin or strong, growing or fading in effectiveness; the longer term value of advertising programs and consumer franchises is ignored; no insight is given to current and future trends in competition, new products, changing tastes, or new uses for old products; patents, technology, proprietary processes, and on-the-job know-how are left out; customer and supplier relationships, employee loyalty, and interdepartmental cooperation are excluded; most of the ingredients required for business success are not represented in accounting reports. Is the "Coke" trademark only worth $1 as stated? Is IBM's marketing capability valueless? Are Jersey Standard's worldwide hydrocarbon reserves of only nominal value? Isn't GM's management its greatest "mark of excellence"? Aren't esprit and imagination the greatest resources of Xerox? Friedrich Krupp was right to have great confidence that his business could quickly be rebuilt even after total, systematic dismemberment by the Allies after World War II; a business is based on people and the Krupp people were ready to rebuild and begin anew. It may not be too severe to say that if financial accounting is the language through which business speaks to investors, then it is a dead language. And the financial analyst who relies on it is at a disadvantage.

There are further problems facing financial analysts, and they should be clearly recognized. At best, financial analysis is an awkward attempt to project future financial patterns working only with past data. (It might be interesting to require management to present their budget for the coming year in annual reports to stockholders. In Canada, prospectuses dealing with natural resources projects must make full projections of management's plans for the future and the expected financial results.)

The financial analyst attempts to build numerical models that fairly represent the company's real business. These models are necessarily dynamic models since the patterns that are to be represented are patterns of business change. The models are built up from the financial relationships between accounting entries. Some of these relationships are constant ratios (e.g., 50 percent of pretax profits go to pay federal income taxes and 50 percent become after-tax earnings). Some are constant absolutes (e.g., the first $1,500,000 of after-tax profits are paid as dividends to preferred stockholders). Some are "positively geared" relationships (e.g., if accelerated depreciation is used for reporting purposes, annual depreciation charges will rise faster than capital expenditures when capital expenditures are increasing). Others are "negatively geared" relationships (e.g., as sales rise, marketing costs rise, but not as rapidly). Some costs are entirely a variable of sales volume (e.g., raw materials); some are semivariable in that they change with the secular trend of sales volume, but not with the year-to-year fluctuations in sales (e.g., distribution facilities). And still other costs are virtually fixed (e.g., rent on the new headquarters office).

The essence of financial analysis is to identify the variables, specify which are independent variables and which others are dependent variables, and then for the dependent variables determine what causes them to change and how much they will change relative to the change in the variable upon which they depend. When the dependencies are internal to the financial model, the analyst's work is relatively easy; when the dependencies are external, the analyst must include such factors as price, cost, competition, and demand. This is not easy.

Two additional major problems face the financial analyst: limited disclosure of data and noncomparability of data dis-

closed in different accounting periods. The usual delays in reporting the financial results of the business are less debilitating. When data is reported only in aggregates (e.g., "sales" can include several thousand products in many unrelated industry categories), the process of aggregation will so blur the realities of the business that only the most naive financial analyst will try to define precise relationships between the aggregates. Essentially, the same analytical adversity comes from the second major problem, the noncomparability of data from period to period. For example, after Polaroid raised $100 million in 1968, the funds were invested in high-yielding municipal bonds. Much of the year-to-year gain in 1969 earnings was due to that interest income—not to new photographic products or increased sales of existing products.

Businesses do change over time, and even a stable business will have changes in the sources of its profits from period to period. (IBM used to be a card-sorting and typewriter company. DuPont used to make gunpowder. And Jersey sold mostly kerosene.) Rapidly growing and dynamic businesses will experience quite dramatic changes in sources of profit. (The conglomerates of 1967 are examples.) The result of not revealing these differences in accounting statements is that relationships are distorted and statistical variance is so great that analytical confidence levels must be very low.

Ratio analysis is most often used by banks and other lenders for rapid and broad surveillance of the financial developments of many companies in an effort to find unusual characteristics, particularly weaknesses, that are worth investigating more carefully. The ease with which this technique raises "questions" does not make it a good source of "answers."

The major advantage of ratios in financial analysis also leads quite often to the main problem with them: ratios are easy to prepare and easy to compare. As a result, they are convenient to use. But, for this same reason, ratios are too often overused. Only a few ratios have important meaning in most analyses. The multitude of additional ratios that can be generated are at best redundant. At worst, they may cause confusion and hide the meaningful ratios from the decision maker. The problem with ratios is that although they give the appearance of high accuracy, most ratios are only gross measures of reality because either the numerator or the denominator—or both—may be distorted.

For example, one of the most commonly used ratios—debt-to-equity—is largely nonsense in a major company. The stockholders' "equity" is usually grossly understated in the accountants' report because the true value of the assets of the corporation are understated. Thus, land, plant, and equipment are carried at "original cost less depreciation and depletion" even though the original cost may be very far below replacement costs and even though amortization may have been taken rapidly. And as we have already noted, the most important corporate assets such as patents, trademarks, customer good will, employee loyalty, executive hustle, research creativity, marketing muscle, and major environmental opportunities for future success are nowhere mentioned. So assets are understated in at least two ways on the balance sheet, and usually substantially so. Since assets minus liabilities equals stockholders' equity, if the assets are understated, then the equity is also understated by an equal dollar amount and a larger, usually much larger, percentage understatement. But if the equity part of the debt/equity ratio is substantially distorted, the ratio will also be distorted. For example, the debt/equity ratio may look like 2:3 when it is really more like 1:10. Ratios must be approached with care and used only sparingly because much of the data input will be inaccurate and therefore the ratio output will be inaccurate even though, by going out to two decimals, giving the false impression of great accuracy.

Despite these caveats, ratio analysis can be useful, particularly in comparing the financial results or position of a company from one reporting period to another. Some of the most useful ratios are the ratio of receivables to sales which shows the turnover or maturity period of accounts receivable; the ratio of sales to materials purchased to measure the value added by the company; and the various ratios of operating costs to sales that can show how and where profitability is being improved or is declining. This analysis aims at discovering the key points of earnings leverage in a company to determine what could go wrong as well as what could go right. For example, if incremental labor costs are low, then volume will be the key to good and bad earnings and marketing is of major importance. But if unit costs of production are high, volume is less important than cost cutting.

While every business is different from every other business, there are always a few key variables that make most of the difference between very good and very bad results. These key variables must be understood. They can be particularly valuable when they help the financial analyst "get inside" the financial system of a company, particularly if they show that short-term factors are temporarily offsetting the positive or negative effects of a long-term trend that does not yet, but soon will, dominate the earnings pattern of the company. For example, are temporary high yields on its municipal bonds hiding a deteriorating position for American Express vis-à-vis the bank credit cards that have been widely introduced in recent years? Have price increases on tax return preparations protected H & R Block's recent earnings from the effects of increasing competition? The first hints at the answers to these questions may come from careful ratio analysis.

Another useful technique is flow-of-funds analysis, which shows the major sources and uses of long-term capital in a company's operations and thus shows the management's financial strategy—whether or not it is a fully intentional strategy. Projections of funds flow can be made under a range of assumptions as to the future business conditions—optimistic, most probable, pessimistic—to provide good estimates of the capital flows over which management has real discretion and those which are really not flexible. For example, an electric utility has less flexibility in its capital expenditures program than an automobile manufacturer would have in its capital program. Flow-of-funds analysis will provide a sound basis for forecasting both the volume and likely financing of new capital requirements, and should help in estimating the type of capital that will be sought by management.

Another technique of financial analysis is called incremental analysis. The basic idea is to determine what happens to every other entry on the Income Statement when Sales rise (or fall) incrementally from one period to another. For example, if Sales go up by an increment of $10 million, what incremental change occurs in Cost of Goods Sold? In Wages and Salaries? In Marketing? In Depletion and Depreciation? In Raw Materials?

Incremental analysis can be used best in analyzing the very short and the very long run changes in the pattern of the Income Statement. Analyzing the rate of change in individual items over a single year or even over a single period can raise useful questions about current operations. Usually these questions take the form of asking whether long-standing relationships in the financial model actually are changing or only appear to be changing because of current, but temporary imbalances.

The long-term use of incremental analysis is to determine major trends in the financial characteristics of the company and hence the investment characteristics of the common stock. Changes in relationships can be set in bold relief by putting the Income Statement for the original and terminal years in percentage terms with Sales set equal to 100 percent, and comparing the weighting of each item with the relative change in each item as shown when change in Sales is also set equal to 100 percent. The objective of this exercise is to identify to what extent and how the potential increase in profits coming from increased revenue was absorbed by increasing costs. What are the "profit leaks"? This analysis may show that the company is either waxing or waning in investment value, and so put the financial analyst in a position to correctly antici-pate the direction and magnitude of future changes in the financial results of the business.

Since the basic problem with financial analysis is usually with the data used, one inescapable conclusion from the dis-cussion in this chapter is that vigorous digging for more and better data can have high returns through improving the basis upon which investment decisions are made.

11

Business analysis

BUSINESS ANALYSIS seeks to understand the true economic nature of a company so that intelligent investments can be made in its common stock. Business analysis and financial analysis must be performed simultaneously; unfortunately, since they are about as different as patting your head while rubbing your stomach, coordinating them is obviously not easy. While financial accounting deals with the symbols of business success and failure, business analysis must deal with the realities that are symbolized.

The concepts and techniques of business analysis that will be described in this chapter may seem straightforward, even obvious. And certainly it is reasonable enough to expect all professional investors to use them regularly and well. But actually they are seldom used effectively. Investors know surprisingly little about the businesses they invest in; what they do know is almost entirely common knowledge, and all too much of this is false. Consequently, business analysis, when it is done well, can be very profitable.

Earnings never change before the business itself changes. And usually a significant change in the pattern of reported earnings will only occur after a relatively long sequence of many kinds of changes in the real business. Xerox management spent years developing the xerographic process before the 914 contributed to earnings. Syntex had a similar experience with steroids. Management consultants who understood the internal squabbling and inadequate planning of the Penn Central management following the merger reliably could predict severe earnings consequences several years before trouble showed in the financials. A new management team at United Fruit had spent several years changing the basic economics of that business before earnings began to rise, lifting the stock nearly 500 percent.

The purpose of business analysis is to *understand and anticipate* the changes in the business that may eventually lead to changes in earnings and therefore in investor expectations—and therefore in the price of the stock. The focus of business analysis is on the few critical factors that could significantly affect long-run investment value. The major *independent* variables must be isolated, analyzed, and understood. On the other hand, financial analysis, as we have already seen, emphasizes the *dependent* variables, one of which is earnings.

The majority of changes in business are due either to external environmental factors over which the company itself has little control, or to changes initiated by the company's own management. So the business analyst must identify the primary independent variables in the environment and forecast changes such as competitive innovations or shifts in market position (IBM-watching in computers); product pricing both on and off list (key to profits in the chemical industry); changes in costs of labor, materials, and purchased components (low-cost TV tubes from Japan); changes in the volume and mix of demand and supply (consumers trading up or down in autos); and so forth. And he must also be alert to management's changes in such factors as the volume, quality, and variety of production (product proliferation in Detroit); shifts in distribution patterns and product promotion (Avon changes its selling cycle from three weeks to two); changes in corporate goals or management emphasis (Aetna decides to become a major life insurer); changes in research and development (DuPont shifts emphasis from new products to new applications for old lines); shifts in employee and union relations (why G.E. took a longer strike than Westinghouse); relations with government regulatory agencies (changes in natural gas price regulation); and relations with suppliers and customers (Studebaker drivers were switching to other brands). Obviously, this is a lot to cover, so the first step is to determine which of these factors can be particularly important and can impact significantly on earnings.

The usual approach to this enormous mission is to ask management a few questions during an occasional, usually rather brief interview. This procedure is at best futile and quite probably will hurt rather than help the investment decision maker because virtually any corporate manager who is experienced at answering investors' questions will be able to give a positive, encouraging, and totally unrealistic series of answers to the obvious questions. He can easily give only the good news, or emphasize the good news and sugarcoat the bad news. (More on this subject follows in Chapter 12.)

The only way to get really important proprietary insights into business problems is through the "scuttlebutt" technique. The most accurate and valuable information any investor would ever want is known right now by customers, suppliers, consultants, employees, former managers, and competitors. Often they know more and know it sooner than top management itself because these are the people who know the company on the firing line where the actual work is being done— not back at headquarters where reports from the field are being read. The scuttlebutt technique involves simply asking these experts what is going on and what is changing and why. They usually can and will tell what they know. This technique works very well for professional spies even in times of war when giving such information on sensitive topics is against the law; it obviously can work well for honest business analysts. (One unusually aggressive investor made a regular practice of bribing the secretaries of two or three top executives or an office boy in any company he owned heavily. He knew more genuine "inside" and timely information than most of the executives in the target companies. Distasteful and reprehensible as this underhanded method is, it does remind us how useful it is to ask the right person the right question at the right time.)

In addition to the direct advantages of legitimate scuttlebutt research—knowing more of what is important and knowing it sooner—the system has an important secondary value. Armed with really good scuttlebutt on one aspect of the business, the business analyst can often show management that he knows the hard realities of that one area and then get better *voluntary* information from management on many other aspects of the company's operations—about which he may actually know far less.

Beyond the gathering and sorting of information, the data must be analyzed for investment significance and then synthesized into a realistic understanding of the nature of the business. For example, financial analysis may show that profit margins have been expanding in recent periods. This result could come from either of two very different causes and therefore have two quite different meanings for investment. If margins are widening because final product prices are higher than normal, or material costs are lower than normal, or volume of production has been unusually high, etcetera, etcetera—then the benefits to earnings growth is essentially nonrecurring because past gains do not necessarily lead directly to further future gains from these same sources. In fact, the gains of the past are likely to be reversed in the future, causing margins to contract back to their normal size. So from an investment decision maker's viewpoint, these are low quality, unsustainable increments to current earnings and have little or no long-term value and really should not affect share prices (although they may do so temporarily). One example: from time to time the amount of property damage due to hurricanes, floods, and the like are below normal because the weather is better than usual in that year, so property and casualty company earnings will be up nicely because margins are temporarily high. But to the long-term investor this means no more than does an occasional bad weather, bad profits year later on. Each is nonrecurring.

On the other hand, if margins are expanding because the mix of goods and services produced by the company is changing for the better because more and more of the company's capacity to produce is being dedicated to higher value-added production of goods and services with strong and sustainable demand, then the recent gains in margins are just a beginning and more margin expansion can be expected. Since regular margin expansion can substantially accelerate earnings growth, this development could greatly increase the investment value and the price of such a company's common stock. Again using property and casualty companies as an example, a few companies are deliberately pruning out their underwriting business, refusing to write unprofitable business even for long-established (but long-unprofitable) customers. The results of this continuing program are higher margins that should continue to widen for several years as the program gets fully implemented.

The business analyst should be able to estimate the magnitude and time sequence of further margin changes. Emphasis on new products which might cause such a rising tide of earnings is readily understandable in this context. However, equal attention should be directed to large volume products that have already matured and may be the cause of shrinking margins and declining investment values. Bristol Myers appears to be having this kind of problem in its Clairol operations. Parke-Davis has had substantial margin pressure in its Chloromycetin product group, a major part of the company's total sales.

Another vital area of business analysis is in the evaluation of management. This sounds trite because it is so often stated as the primary function of investment decision making. Unfortunately, very, very few investors understand the real capabilities of even one management group. In very large companies it is probably impossible to evaluate management on any criteria other than past profit performance, because a very large company essentially runs itself with so much momentum and ingrained habit that top management can rarely change any major part of the operation in less than a decade. Investors should remember President John F. Kennedy's lament when replying to a bold new proposal during his administration: "I agree with you, but will the government?" or Sergeant Brandt: "The officers come and the officers go, but the Troop remains the same."

Small companies, on the other hand, can be and are changed by management, often by one or two primary personalities in the management group. In these companies, the study of the principal managers, their working relationships, their strengths and weaknesses, their personal and business goals and motives, and even their personal lives can be of great importance to a judgment on the long-term investment value of their company. A small company can never become more successful than its key managers aspire to make it. In small and medium-sized companies, a change in a key manager's role can have major investment significance, and the business analyst should be able to anticipate those results by knowing the people involved.

Another aspect of management evaluation arises during what might best be called corporate adolescence: the period of transition from a small company to a large one when new concepts, methods, and managerial skills must be brought into the company if it is to sustain its growth and momentum. Many companies stumble during this period; some fail altogether. Mattel, which some investors wrongly saw as a small-time toy company with a hot fad in Barbie Doll has proven very successful at becoming a large company. The capacity for such growth was in the founders' sense of the business potential and in their ability to guide the company from a proprietorship to a professional management. The business analyst should try to anticipate for each company when this transition period will begin and how the particular company will fare in the changeover.

Returning now to analysis of large companies, even if their managements cannot be usefully analyzed on a man-by-man basis, an important piece of business analysis is well worth undertaking. Every large, well-established company develops a distinctive culture within its ranks. Group norms of behavior develop. Business style grows more and more elaborate. The corporate mission becomes widely accepted. Work habits, dress, manners, office space, and so forth all become accustomed general characteristics of the company. The tests and prerequisites of success become standardized. The tempo of activity is steady. Decision criteria and values are defined. Internal politics are stabilized and become refined. All of this and more makes up the company culture and character. It will largely determine the company's behavior in various kinds of environments. These are the things management cannot quickly change. The investor who understands the real nature of a company will be able to avoid all the problems that other investors make for themselves by believing that so-and-so or such-and-such will somehow change the company significantly. Only major change can shift the direction and pace of a company that has adapted itself to one direction and pace over long periods of time. Corporations, like nations, are culturally determined.

Major business change can come with major investment significance to a large company from four major sources: management-ownership change; technological change; environmental change; and change that comes as a unique occurrence, such as the discovery of natural resources. The basic task is to determine the magnitude and the timing of the impact of these major changes on earnings, and this simply cannot be done through financial analysis. Since the investment significance, whether positive or negative, will usually be fully reflected in common stock price changes before the results of these changes will be fully reflected in financial statements, evaluation of these changes obviously depends upon business analysis. Of the several types of major change, the one that most warrants specific discussion here is change in ownership and/or management, particularly when effected through acquisition.

Most mergers do not represent "action by two strong and self-sufficient companies seeking to achieve synergistic benefits through a healthy combination of strengths that will significantly benefit their shareholders." Most mergers have as their common denominator the recognition by at least one management that it is not, for various reasons, well prepared to succeed in the future. (See Mace and Montgomery's *Management Problems of Corporate Acquisitions*, for extensive documentation on this proposition.)

Second, most managements know very little about the business realities of the companies they are considering merging with. At best, management will "take a look at the books" of the other company. But this is only the past, and the future is what has frightened the merger into being. Far too few acquisition-oriented managements seem to realize that a merger or acquisition involves a very long term, very expensive, very illiquid investment decision to buy the stock of the other company, a momentous decision that warrants unusually thorough and broad-ranging investment analysis and business analysis. The 1969 and 1970 problems of the 1967 and 1968 conglomerates bear this thought out.

Third, most acquisitions and mergers are so structured as to "look good" to investors at the start. Tender offers are always made above the market. Dividends are often higher after the deal than before. Book values and earnings are often increased. Growth rates usually are somewhat enhanced. But this apparent improvement deals only with accounting reports and financial analysis; it is merely symbolic logic. The business analyst must look to the fit of the people, the markets, the technologies, the financial needs and resources, and so on, to determine whether there is a valid business logic for a given merger or acquisition that increases the value rather than just the price of his investment—because price increases are not self-sustaining.

Probably the worst kind of merger in terms of its impact on long-term investment value occurs when a company whose shares are valued in terms of its *assets* merges with a company whose shares are valued in terms of its growth in *earnings*. At first, these arrangements always look good and attractive: the growth company will have more assets to employ creatively and the asset company will have more dynamic management, and so investors expect to see faster real growth in earnings and a multiplied gain in share value as the price earnings ratio rises. It doesn't work that way for long. In fact, the usual result is the reverse of what was expected. Managements capable of developing highly profitable uses of capital have never been much restricted by lack of money, so the influx of redundant capital doesn't make much difference to their ability to generate good business opportunities and growth in earnings. The management's skill, imagination, and drive are the real sources of earnings growth, so with more shares sharing each increment of management-created growth the per share earnings growth usually slows noticeably. Meanwhile, the per share asset values have been divided among so many more shares that this is usually no longer an adequate support to the share prices. As a result, the probabilities are that the asset-and-growth merger will cross-sterilize rather than cross-fertilize the constituent companies and that the long-term investment results will be adverse. Leasco's acquisition of Reliance Insurance—and the subsequent drop in share prices—exemplifies this point. Per share assets were too low to support the old Reliance price, and growth was too slow to hold up Leasco. In analyzing mergers, as in every phase of business analysis, the objective is to gain an advantageous perspective on the symbols of financial reporting by understanding the business realities that underlie the financial statements.

Whatever techniques are used, the *sine qua non* of business analysis is gathering significant information. Most of this information will be qualitative, whereas the financial data is largely quantitative. But without these qualitative insights into the real nature of the business, the quantitative data will be easily misunderstood. A useful way to express the difference between financial and business analysis is that financial analysis deals with *knowledge* that has a rapid rate of obsolescence and requires continuous and extensive maintenance, while business analysis strives for an *understanding* that is harder to develop but is much longer lasting in terms of investment usefulness and also requires less frantic maintenance effort.

The purpose of business analysis is to breathe life and

substance into financial analysis so that the investor can avoid problems and pursue opportunities. Sound business analysis is the basic building block of successful investing, particularly for the large institutional portfolios which are the concern of this book. Unfortunately, this is also perhaps the only area of investment management that cannot be taught and even possibly cannot be learned because it depends almost entirely on the individual analyst's ability to form sound qualitative judgments on a wide variety of delicate issues, and on his personal motivation to hustle for extra information and insight.

12

Analytical pitfalls

SOME OF THE comments in the several preceding chapters on analysis may have suggested that this part of professional investing is relatively easy. It's not. Research-and-analysis is the hardest and toughest part of professional investing. Effective investment analysis would make everything else in this business easy. Unfortunately, investment analysis is fraught with many dangers that fully challenge even the most gifted and experienced analyst to find a safe passage to a sound conclusion. While it is no more feasible to explain in this chapter exactly what *not* to do than it has been feasible in previous chapters to explain exactly what must be done to be successful in analysis, at least a few observations can be made on the general nature of analytical pitfalls and pratfalls. Explaining the most frequent errors may help others to avoid repeating them as frequently as their predecessors have.

The most common reason for failure in investment analysis is inadequate care and effort. This usually shows up as excessive emphasis on financial analysis and inadequate attention to business analysis. Even worse, there is a natural tendency to allow a research-and-analysis mission to deteriorate into simple reporting. And the reporting is usually based upon what management has to say about the company's position and its future. And this is very thin ice for the serious investor.

Management does not tell the bad news. There are many reasons why investors cannot rely upon management to describe the problems that keep corporate executives awake at night. First, the "line" executives expect or hope to overcome the business problems before they develop into significant investment problems; managers solve potential disasters many times each year and a positive, "can do" attitude is usually critical to executive achievement. Second, normal business problems only become unusual investment problems "at the last minute," just as they explode out of control. Third, managers often honestly believe they are on the right course and doing their best when they are actually heading for serious trouble. How can investors expect managers to see the error of their own ways when, despite their best efforts, they are actually in the process of making a mistake? Finally, in some cases, management can and will deliberately lie to investment analysts, especially when boosting or holding up share prices would help in closing a major deal.

Most investors who rely on management sources for investment information rely specifically on a financial officer who has been assigned the task of maintaining stockholder relations. This is seldom a manager of real importance to the company's future despite possibly impressive titles; if he were really important, he would have a different job. Because this officer is seldom involved in the critical phases of management's work, he usually relies upon information volunteered to him by the line officers who naturally tend to emphasize their achievements and aspirations rather than their shortcomings and anxieties. His view of the corporation, therefore, is through rose colored glasses.

In addition, he deals primarily with the financial record of past development, because most of the investors he communicates with concentrate on financial questions. And his view tends to be out the rear window of the corporate vehicle. The result is that the financial relations officer is often the last executive to get the word about significant positive or negative changes in the business. And like almost all investors and almost all executives, he will usually underestimate adversity. Without ever intending to do anything other than a fair and careful job, this principal source of information for investors all too often finds himself playing the unhappy role of the judas goat. Unrealistic dependency on him by analysts is the most common trap in investment decision making.

A very different analytical pitfall comes from not recognizing the real and sometimes substantial differences between the time cycle of investors and the time cycle of corporate management. This difference shows up in many ways. For the long-term good of the company and its owners, management elects to take a labor strike to win important freedom to use labor-saving equipment and so increase future earnings; the response of the institutional investor is to sell the stock down to lower prices because current quarterly earnings will suffer. (The so-called Boulware Strike at General Electric was a typical example.) Or a major new product innovation is discovered; the shares are bid up in anticipation of future benefits and then decline as investors grow impatient with the long lead time required to introduce a sophisticated new product, even though the product development schedule is being fully met by the company. (IBM's stock shot up when the 360 series of computers was first announced, but slumped to an historically low relative P/E before the first machines rolled off the assembly lines ahead of schedule.) Usually, the problem is that corporate time is measured in years and decades while investment time is measured in days and months. Analysts who evaluate corporate developments without giving consideration to the time frame of the equity market will experience unnecessary losses.

Another analytical pitfall is to do unbalanced analysis, making the investment judgment on factors internal to the company and giving too little weight to its business environment or the stock market. R. J. Reynolds' earnings and dividends rose in every year of the 1960s, but due to investor concern about smoking and health, the shares stayed in the low 40s throughout most of the decade. It was not a buy.

A related problem involves overlooking the seemingly unimportant parts of a company's total business, and then having that "small" operation suffer a major adversity and seriously affect the profits of business as a whole and hence depress the share prices as investors react to disappointment. How many investors knew or cared that Owens Illinois had sugar operations in the Caribbean until problems there caused a quarterly drop in earnings? This sort of trap is sprung surprisingly often.

Another problem is to build a case that is too complex, one that requires too many variables to go the "right way." The bulls on LTV in 1968 at prices of $130 a share came a cropper for this reason. Simplicity is important in investing. And a wide tolerance for error and inaccuracy is usually necessary for an investment decision to prove successful. Complex future projections do not often come true.

In a quite different area, analysts can be ambushed by market forces. There is in almost all investors a great tendency to "fall in love" with stocks, particularly *after* a stock has produced important portfolio profits. Unfortunately, a stock is always rising in price just before it reaches its once-in-a-decade "high." There is a curious tendency, as share prices rise, for investors to raise their earnings and growth estimates and to revise upwards their evaluation of management, the business of the company, and its independence from external forces. This tendency lies behind two different analytical pitfalls: the analyst may be tempted to raise his expectations in order to justify the higher stock price, only to be disappointed later as more realistic results unfold. Or he may hold to his original expectations of earnings, later to be personally gratified when these expectations are confirmed by actual results, and then be surprised to see the share price abruptly decline as *other* investors react with disappointment to actual earnings because these other investors have inflated *their* expectations and are now disappointed with the sober realities.

Another kind of "market related" pitfall is forgetting how important market valuation of stocks and bonds can be to a corporation that regularly needs more capital to finance its growth. Clearly an acquisition-oriented company can make much more profitable deals if it has a high P/E stock. (The conglomerates of the late sixties were an extreme example of the power of the high P/E). Or, to take another example, builders and building materials suppliers depend upon the volume and cost of mortgage money to finance construction. The major slump in this industry in 1968–70 was not due to inadequate demand, but to inadequate mortgage money. These capital market pitfalls are cyclical; another type is really secular in that its impact is felt over a much longer term.

The electric utilities and telephone companies enjoyed an impressive P/E multiple level in the late fifties and early sixties for two reasons: demand was growing steadily, and their allowed rates of return were far above the costs of long-term debt. This last element was critical. In a sense, the common stockholders were capitalizing on the low cost of debt. But later in the decade as interest rates rose sharply —without fully offsetting increases in allowed rates of return

—equity investors got squeezed. Instead of earnings growing faster because debt was cheap, earnings growth was slowed because debt was expensive—particularly when 2.5 percent bonds were refinanced at 8 percent! As EPS growth slowed, P/E multiples also sagged. This meant that it took more shares of stock to raise, say, $10 million of equity for new plant and equipment needed to meet still growing demand. Since more shares had to be sold, the total earnings were divided among more shares, which also cut down EPS growth. The lower P/Es were reducing EPS growth, which in turn reduced the P/Es, which cut EPS growth, and so on. During the decade of the 1960s, utilities made for very poor investments as a direct result of this changed pattern vis-à-vis the capital markets.

A common problem of over- or underestimating earnings, particularly among newer analysts, is the result of placing too much emphasis upon quantitative analysis and paying too little attention to the qualitative character of a company, its business, and the people who make it move. The strengths or the weaknesses of the people who form a company are more powerful than many tyro analysts believe possible: superior managers will go well ahead of what might be expected from "by the numbers" analysis, and poor managers will almost always disappoint the analyst who relies too heavily upon quantitative projections.

Some more specific analytical pitfalls are worth noting. Companies that market consumer products are quite different from industrial companies. When an industrial company launches a major new product, most of the costs are capital costs such as depreciation of new plants and equipment, and will be amortized over the life of the product being produced. In consumer companies, on the other hand, the costs are usually items treated as a current expense such as advertising, promotion, sampling, and so on, and are charged against earnings as incurred. Hence the difference: in a consumer products company, the introduction of a major new product can severely depress or disrupt earnings, particularly when the costs of building a market that will be profitably exploited for many years in the distant future are all charged against only a few months of current earnings. In a very real sense, the cost of investing for the future comes from the Income Statement in a consumer products company rather than from the balance sheet as in an industrial company. The analytical problem is to know when this "investment spending" is relatively high and when it is relatively low because earnings growth will be the mirror image of this development spending, with earnings "growing" faster when product/market development is "growing" more slowly. For example, in the mid-1960s General Foods accelerated its new product development expenditures after a several year period of slower product introductions. This action hurt current earnings until the "new product backlog" was filled up and development expenditures could be normalized. Then earnings began to grow at a more rapid rate than before, and the stock price responded accordingly.

Another specific pitfall is usually found in high-margin consumer products such as drugs which are often manufactured in anticipation of a new demand in the marketplace. In the case of new and sophisticated drugs, the product may be manufactured, packaged, labeled, and crated, ready for shipment, waiting only for final approval by the Food and Drug Administration. Unfortunately, on some occasions the necessary FDA approval has been delayed weeks and even months so that shipment was postponed with a resultant severe shortfall in quarterly earnings, followed by a stock price collapse. This problem hurt a pharmaceutical subsidiary of North American Phillips in 1968. The company had developed, produced, packaged, and even taken orders for a new vaccine.

When FDA's approval to ship the product was not received on schedule, actual earnings fell far below expectations and the stock reacted quickly. Finished goods inventories, the difference between production and shipments, have tripped up many investors in many kinds of companies.

Cancerous growth, a current mushrooming of earnings that almost necessarily will lead to a future collapse in earnings, is still another problem. Companies that come into a market to serve an acute, but limited demand (such as computer leasing) can show unusually rapid period-to-period earnings gains until the available market becomes satiated and then their business deteriorates abruptly because they have not developed a really viable future, having cannibalized their limited market opportunity to show swift short-term results. Companies with a known horizon or terminus should never be valued as growth companies.

Time and again investors misunderstand the true source of earnings growth in a company and assume that reported gains in earnings are being produced by one product which is quite exotic when, in fact, the gains are actually coming from a quite different, often very mundane product. When all the excited talk about Syntex in the early sixties had to do with birth control and steroid chemistry, the earnings were actually coming from an effective, but far from exotic salve. As a result of this sort of misunderstanding, investors sometimes place an unusually high price/earnings valuation on the company's achievements only to be subsequently disappointed when mundane earnings are achieved by the mundane product.

Investors can easily be confused by companies actively involved in acquisitions, and misinterpret the reasons for gains in earnings. Particularly if the management is bright and articulate, investors may ascribe postmerger margin gains to value-adding by management when most of the gains are actually coming from cost cutting and so, as we have seen in a previous chapter, are essentially nonrecurring. Since a company's earnings are usually accorded a higher price/earnings multiple when investors generally believe value-adding is increasing its margins and its growth, an acquisition-active, cost-cutting company can make more frequent and more attractive acquisitions if it is *misunderstood*. But only so long as it is misunderstood, because proper appraisal will result in a lower multiple, which will retard acquisitions, which will retard earnings increments, which will further penalize the multiple. This can be very depressing, particularly on the stock price.

There are many many ways in which investors can be wrong. This chapter has only indicated some of the most common mistakes. Investors operate in a turbulent field affected by many complex forces. And they have their own limitations as individuals. The best they can hope for is to learn enough from their own mistakes and the mistakes of others to reduce the frequency and magnitude of their future mistakes.

13

Risk analysis
and management

THE TITLE of this chapter has been chosen quite deliberately: among investors "risk" is often discussed, but seldom analyzed with care. The overall result is that risk is usually considered only in retrospect when it should really be considered only in prospect. Properly analyzed, risk can be measured and understood. And if risk can be measured and understood, it can be managed to increase long-term portfolio profits.

Risk has been given so many meanings in so many circumstances that it can be discussed usefully only by individually exploring a variety of issues subsumed under the single term "risk." This chapter undertakes to sort out and rationalize this fascinating subject and to set forth a sound approach to risk analysis and management. We begin with portfolio risk then cover risk in individual stocks, and then comment on what might best be called client risks. Each type of risk is really quite different from the others, and must be managed in a different way.

142

The key to understanding risk is to separate long-term risk from short-term risk. Long-term risk—for the investor who can wait long enough to see stock prices in their long-term pattern—is the risk of low or even negative long-term returns. Short-term risk is the variability of prices seen close up on a daily, weekly, or monthly basis. The two types of risk are shown in the accompanying illustration.

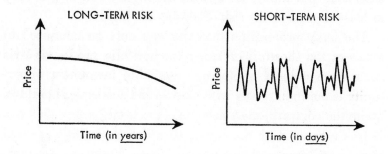

In the very short run, investors have great difficulty reading the long-term trend of price when those prices have great short-term variability. But, as we will discover in the following passages, stocks with the greatest long-term risk often have low interim price variability or short-term risk while stocks with considerable short-term risk characteristics often have the best long-term prospects. This is particularly true when many individually volatile stocks are combined into large, diversified, long-term portfolios. (See Chapter 5.)

For a large, well-diversified, long-term portfolio, actual investment risk is the degree to which that portfolio fails to achieve over the long term a rate of return that is average or normal for the type of investments available to it. This failure to keep pace with the averages can occur in either of two ways: below-average profits earned or above-average losses incurred. (Excessive costs of management is another possibility.) Most people measure portfolio risk only in terms of the above-average losses, but the opportunity costs of profits foregone can be just as important. A $10 million shortfall in a large institutional portfolio is no less a shortfall simply because it was never earned than if it were once held and then lost. An investment policy that avoids the risk of large losses almost automatically incurs the risk of missing large profits. Consequently, in establishing basic investment policy for institutional portfolios, the risk of aiming too low is probably at least as great as the risk of aiming too high.

The basic proposition that risk can only be measured in terms of the shortfall of long-term portfolio profits vis-à-vis some measurement of average available investment opportunity is not in harmony with most of the academic literature. Quite the contrary, most academicians would argue that risk is best measured by the degree to which a portfolio's actual returns are *greater* than—not *less* than—the average return. They would explain their view this way: "Since the investment markets tend to be perfectly competitive, prices at any point in time will fairly reflect both the problems and opportunities inherent in each stock or group of stocks, and therefore if one portfolio earns higher than average profits, it axiomatically must have accepted equally higher than average chances of losses. . . ." So they say in academe. They say "the above-average risk incurred to achieve above-average gains is exactly equal to the above-average profits earned." In other words, incremental profit equals incremental risk. Now since most academicians measure risk in terms of price volatility, one could say that this argument is just further support for the view expressed in Chapter 5 that volatile stocks make superior portfolios because substituting "volatility" for "risk," we can summarize again saying: incremental profit equals incremental volatility and vice versa.

The problem seems to stem from confusion about risk as opposed to uncertainty. In formal terms, risk involves a situation about which the various possible outcomes and their respective probabilities of occurrence are *known to the decision maker at the time he makes his decision.* Uncertainty, on the other hand, involves a situation about which the probabilities of the possible outcomes are *not* known. In investment management, particularly over the short and intermediate term, it is uncertainty (not risk) that characterizes such factors as stock prices. This uncertainty is most clearly measured in terms of stock price volatility—the degree to which an individual stock price changes by more or by less than the change in average stock prices—because price volatility is due to investor uncertainty about long-term value.

But, as we have seen in the discussion of equity portfolio policy in Chapter 5, a large, diversified, long-term fund of volatile stocks should earn an above-average rate of return. The same result has been found true for bonds: for large, well-diversified portfolios, lower grade bonds produced higher returns than did high-grade bonds. In other words, uncertainty does not equal long-term risk. And in fact, uncertainty about stocks and bonds has been greater than actual risk. And this is precisely why volatile (uncertain) stocks will earn above-average returns in institutional portfolios over the long haul.

As we have seen in Chapter 7, it is essential to distinguish between the "riskiness" of a stock in isolation and the "riskiness" of the same stock in the context of a large, well-diversified portfolio. The sum of the individual stock risks is *not* equal to the portfolio's risk. This is simply because for some stocks in a well-developed portfolio, a particular stimulus will be negative, while for others the impact will be positive. As a result, over time the unusual gains will offset the unusual losses. Without intending to belabor the point, at the portfolio level the risk of experiencing an actual loss in one stock is neither less nor more significant than the risk of missing an equally large profit opportunity in another issue. In other words, while risk is usually thought of only in terms of a loss in a single stock, it must be considered in dual terms—unexpected gain *and* unexpected loss—when analyzing the risk of that same stock in a portfolio.

This returns us to the important subject of diversification, which is the primary method of managing risk. Diversification has two purposes. The first purpose (Type A) is to combine in a single portfolio several different types of stocks; different in the way their prices and earnings respond to major shifts in the economic environment. For example, one type of stock (such as banks) might show higher earnings during tight money periods while another type of stock (such as home builders) might show lower earnings during such a period. The objective of this Type A diversification is to reduce the volatility of the portfolio as a whole when compared to the volatility of its component stocks by matching, grouping, or pairing stocks that will have divergent price responses to a common future stimulus. Having determined how to balance such pairs, the portfolio manager can build a more-efficient-than-average portfolio by seeking either lower volatility for a given rate of return or a higher rate of return for a given level of volatility.

The second purpose of diversification (Type B) is to identify groups of stocks that should behave the *same* way in response to changes in the environment, and then invest in them *as a group* or as a subportfolio. Investing in a group of similar stocks is a way to self-insure against unexpected developments in just one or two companies that might be chosen from a group and to obtain for the portfolio the expected average return for that type of stock. (This ties back to earlier discussion of the advantages of strategy over selection of individual issues.) For example, if electric utilities were identified as attractive for investment for basic reasons having to do with major developments in that industry, it would be wiser to invest in several companies operating in different parts of the country than to invest in just one company and thereby run the risk of unexpected poor weather conditions in that one region defeating the investment purpose. Or if a stock-market-oriented strategic decision were made to invest in high-growth companies, sound Type B diversification practice would favor acquiring several different stocks having the desired high-growth characteristics rather than risking the success of the whole strategy on a single company which might run into special problems and not behave as expected.

The two purposes of diversification can be achieved simultaneously by pairing groups of stocks expected to respond differently to environmental factors. For example, a group of banks might be paired with a group of home building companies so that average experience with one group is balanced with average experience in the other group as interest rates change and impact on both groups.

Three real risks or problems are potentially involved in diversification procedure, although careful management can largely remove them. The first problem is tantamount to loss of control over the stocks in the portfolio simply because the number of stocks in the fund exceeds the manager's capacity to understand fully what is developing in each situation. This would prevent the manager from adding value through his selection of specific stocks or groups and may leave him prey to superficial reasoning and emotional reactions to the market behavior of the various stocks. He can quite simply get "spread too thin."

The other risk involved in diversification is to achieve apparent, but false, diversification. This has been a common problem, usually associated with so-called industry-by-industry diversification in which a portfolio holding auto stocks would also have glass, rubber, and steel stocks, supposedly for diversification and balance. But, if autos hit hard times, the same would be true of the glass, rubber, and steel companies that depend so much upon large volume sales to the auto companies. Consequently, these companies' stocks are essentially a class or group and will usually rise and fall together. This might achieve a modicum of Type B diversification, but is not the Type A diversification usually intended and expected.

A third problem in diversifying a portfolio is to use a stock because of its *past* characteristics and not recognize that it has changed its price characteristics or earnings pattern. The result of this mistaken identity is that the stock behaves contrary to expectation and may hurt rather than help the balance of the portfolio. This problem is far more subtle and rare than the other two, but it is at least as important. The most common ways in which the behavior of earnings can be changed is through merger with another company in a quite different kind of business or through product maturity in a major line. Price behavior can be changed by shifts in the nature of the supply of shares, the demand for shares, or both. The most common example of changes in supply/demand relationships is when large aggressive institutions begin rapidly buying into a stock whose market is usually dominated by more conservative investors. The example of Anaconda (Chapter 9) was just such a case. Fortunately, changes in the characteristic behavior of stocks can be monitored and appropriate response taken by investment managers.

A few more types of risk at the portfolio level should be noted here. The "transaction risk" is that market liquidity in a stock or group of stocks will be inadequate for prompt execution of a purchase or sale, usually the latter, and that a heavy price discount or price premium will be required to clear the desired transaction. The "market risk" is that a stock is overpriced relative to value, that this is becoming more and more widely recognized, that past price behavior will therefore not continue, and that a major loss will be experienced while a new price-to-value relationship is being worked out. The "timing risk" is trying to outguess the short-term swings in market prices, trying to buy low and sell high. The "turnover risk" is trying to make too many short-term moves and not being able to make that many decisions very well. The "major moves risk" is attempting to shift from one market to another without the special expertise required on both markets to know when such a shift would offer a worthwhile advantage. This "major move" can be from one type of security to another such as from stocks to bonds or from stocks to cash; or it can be within a market such as from highly volatile stocks to low-volatility stocks; or it can be made from the American stock market to the Japanese stock market. As discussed in Chapters 3 and 4, the chance for error is very great in such moves; the magnitude of potential profit is seldom substantial. Such risk is best avoided altogether. While it is possible for a portfolio to make money in the short run by taking these portfolio risks, it does not appear feasible to achieve sustained superior performance over the long term. These are real risks that result in real losses— even if it takes a little time for "the punishment to fit the crime."

Last among the various portfolio level risks is trying too hard, particularly in the final stages of a major bull market. At the market top, the rate of return required to justify the high prices is so very high that only speculative stocks could conceivably meet the market's high hurdle rate. So in an effort to continue to "earn" high rates of return, some fund managers go in for the most speculative issues. Often, they buy and sell so rapidly that they are really just trading. And they are making so very many decisions that the quality of decisions drops off sharply. Of course, the high volume of trading in these stocks may give the appearance of pretty good liquidity, but when the panic finally starts there are no buyers around, prices collapse, and the losses are very real. This is such an obvious trap to experienced investors that it should be easy to avoid this risk altogether.

Following this discussion of risk analysis and risk management at the portfolio level, it will serve our purposes well to recall some of the kinds of risk that relate to individual stocks (in addition to those problems covered in Chapter 12). Accounting practices can be changed, sometimes in ways that are complete surprises even to management. For example, in 1969, Career Academy was pressured into changing its method of accounting for franchises with the result that reported earnings were abruptly cut in half and the stock fell to less than a third of its former price—even though the business itself did not change. Such changes can be mandated by the Accounting Principles Board of the American Institute of Certified Public Accountants or by the Securities and Exchange Commission. (For example, in 1970 the basis for accounting for mergers and acquisitions was almost completely changed.) For stocks whose price is a function of per share earnings, such shifts in accounting can be a major source of price risk.

When the price/earnings multiple drops, the stock price will also fall unless earnings go up by even more than the multiple drops. For example, if the P/E drops down 20 percent, the EPS would have to be up 25 percent to maintain the stock price. This P/E risk usually shows up in a gradual deterioration of P/E sapping the strength out of otherwise satisfactory progress in earnings.

Obviously, dividends can be cut, and where current yield is the basic price support, this can be a major risk.

Laws, regulations, and government practices (even expropriation) can also represent significant risk. For example, in 1964 the Mexican government withdrew Pan American Sulphur's sulphur export permit and the stock lost 60 percent in a few days. The same is true of new inventions or services by competitors that may truncate a company's sales and earnings. (Lockheed's Constellation was an enormous success until Boeing and Douglas began producing commercial jet aircraft.) Strikes, price wars, start-up expenses, and a host of other operating problems can pose investment risk for an individual stock. (Examples here are literally legion.) The list could be extended for many pages, but this is enough to support these points: for each stock every major problem possibility should be identified, its potential impact should be quantified explicitly, and its probability specified.

Portfolio managers cannot manage individual stock uncertainties efficiently unless they are carefully analyzed and presented in a convenient form (ideally summarized on a single page). As time passes, the elements of risk and their probability of occurrence will change—sometimes substantially—so the analysis of these risks should be reviewed at regular intervals, and changes in the risk/reward balance should be carefully considered to determine whether action should be taken. Only by carefully developing a clear understanding of the specific character of each element of uncertainty can the composite "riskiness" of a stock be usefully understood. Without this breakdown of uncertainty, vague generalizations will be all too easily accepted, thus precluding sound management of risk.

In discussing risk in stocks and in portfolios, we have carefully insisted on separating risk from uncertainty, but in turning now to client risk, the two come back together. Volatility of prices due to uncertainty may not equate to risk over the long term, but it can equal real risk for clients. This can happen by removing the essential feature of the portfolios discussed in this book—their long-term character. Up to this point, we have brushed aside the interim fluctuations in both individual stocks and in the portfolio as a whole because over the long term such fluctuations will be quite unimportant. But, for any individual or organization obliged to "settle up" and close his account at a particular moment, the supposedly nominal interim decline in prices can be frozen into actual loss. This problem of supposedly short-term price fluctuations potentially becoming long-term capital losses is most apparent in managing investments for individual clients who will someday die. It can also be important for some types of employee benefit plans (see Chapter 18). And it can be a critical problem for the individual or organization who may be forced to withdraw and spend capital just at the time when the portfolio has taken a strong cyclical decline in price.

One of the major recurring causes of inferior investment returns is responding to short-term uncertainty rather than to long-term probabilities, and being improperly conservative, often at the most inopportune times. The other major recurring theme of inferior returns is getting overextended and not having enough capital or enough independence from current spending needs to be able to wait out a bad market period. In brief, fear and greed are the main causes of client troubles. Investors should be careful to do two things: first, invest in long-term portfolios only those assets that will not be needed near term, while putting aside a reserve of capital that may be needed near term, and then not allow near-term considerations to disrupt sound practices and policies for long-term purposes.

Prudent, profitable risk-taking depends upon three different kinds of resources: time resources, financial resources, and emotional resources. Investors can take greater risk if they can wait longer for their reward, if they do not need to call upon the invested money to pay current bills, and if they have more intestinal fortitude when the going gets rough. Fortunately for the perfect investor, most other investors' actions are dominated by impatience, tight budgets, and weak nerves. And even for those who do not suffer all three deficiencies, the one resource that is in shortest supply is the factor that will govern their investment behavior.

Risk, by the way, does not equal opportunity. While greater risk and price volatility are almost always associated with great investment opportunity, the reverse is not necessarily true. Aggressively seeking greater and greater risks on the naive presumption that greater rewards would somehow follow automatically is what led to the ruination of many a go-go fund manager in the late sixties.

This chapter has emphasized the many facets of risk because only after cataloguing all the many ways in which risk appears in individual stocks and in aggregate portfolios can the investment manager and his client attempt to manage these risks. In addition, emphasis has been given to a critical factor in risk analysis and management: although most of us think of risk as a negative event, the unexpected change *can* be either positive or negative. It seems clear that the essence of risk management in a portfolio is to balance the chances of good and bad breaks through sound diversification procedures. And the key to risk management in individual stocks is to identify the potential problems early and be prepared to react promptly to negative developments. Finally, the first rule to follow in managing client risk (and stock and portfolio risk) is to refuse to take really big risks. Risks should be taken on purpose with a clear understanding of the possible positive or negative consequences. The risk-taker should know what he is doing and why he is doing it. Reasonable, moderate, deliberate risks are easy to manage. No risk should ever be taken if it might cause permanent harm.

14

Market analysis

MARKET ANALYSIS is concerned entirely with prices and markets. It attempts to answer the following kinds of questions: Does the present price of a stock equal, exceed, or fall below its investment value? Is the quoted price real, i.e., could a large transaction be executed at or near that price? How are the forces of demand and supply changing? How will prices change? How liquid is the market? How does each particular stock relate to the market as a whole? These are difficult questions to answer; market price judgment is an area of little science. The best that most institutional investors can hope for in this area is to avoid a few major market traps each year and also to raise some important market-oriented questions about the structure and composition of their portfolios.

There is a strong natural tendency among human beings to try to find order in their environment in order to gain control over it, and much of the history of human advancement can be realistically traced to this strong motivation. Unfortunately, when men do not find order in their environment, they often invent an ersatz ordering and impose it upon the data available to them. In recent years, natural scientists have found our environment to be far more complex, subtle, intricate, and dynamic than had previously been supposed, and so they are striving to be less mechanistic in their view of the universe. This is not true of stock market technicians who try to read precise meaning from the volume and price patterns of individual equities, groups of stocks, and the market as a whole. Very few institutional investors have found these studies consistently helpful in picking stocks and increasing the number of winners among the stocks in their portfolios. On the other hand, they are almost always helpful when used to focus the portfolio manager's attention on the stern realities of market prices, force him to question each stock's role in the fund, and so help reduce portfolio losses. Of course, fewer losses means that more of the profits are kept and that makes the total portfolio return higher. So it is important to appreciate the ways in which technical studies can be most helpful. They provide a watchdog service, making noises when things don't look right. They ask *questions* ("The market is moving against this stock: are you *sure* you want to own it?"). They do not provide definite answers.

The evidence produced by a series of extensive statistical tests of various quantitative techniques for screening and selecting stocks based upon market price behavior consistently supports the view that information about past prices and past volume of trading will not help investors make better estimates of future prices. The scholars who have studied this subject summarize their findings by saying stock prices are a "random walk." In other words, the Dow Theory does not work because past prices do not predict future prices. Buying or selling on high or low volume or on rising or falling prices or any of the possible combinations and permutations is futile. It does not work. The evidence that technical analysis of individual stocks is useless is overwhelming. Almost any technique may work for awhile, but none works for long. To paraphrase Robert Frost, technicians dance round in a ring and suppose; the market sits in the middle and knows. (But it's not telling.)

Another approach to analyzing market prices takes a broad "macro" approach—studies the intermediate and longer term trend of the overall market—and *can* be unusually powerful as a basic frame of reference around which to build a market-oriented strategy. But, for most investors, evaluation of the "market outlook" is more qualitative than quantitative. They tend to form broad judgments on equally broad generalizations about such weighty topics as political conditions at home and abroad, social and demographic trends, the condition of the domestic economy and the soundness of the dollar overseas, and put particular emphasis on "investor psychology." From all these ingredients, like the witches in *MacBeth*, they declare the stock market to be bullish or bearish. Sociable and entertaining? Yes, but not very helpful to sustained portfolio performance. Fortunately, there is a better way.

For years, economists have argued that for *any* market, the level of prices is determined by supply and demand seeking out a mutually satisfactory price-level equilibrium. Applying this simple concept to the market for stocks leads to a new and quite different approach to forecasting the overall stock market price level and direction through analysis of changes in the supply and demand for common stocks.

This new approach is considerably more useful and more profitable than the previous approach because it is now possible to undertake a serious forecast of the probable direction and magnitude of equity price changes in much the same way similar forecasts are made for the bond market using the Federal Reserve Board's flow of funds data on the year-to-year changes in the supply of and demand for credit.

The analysis of supply and demand in the equity market includes many rather stable secular trends such as the growth in corporate and public pension funds as pension obligations increase, or the growth in mutual funds as a result of increases in discretionary income, and some very unstable, cyclical factors such as the changes in demand for U.S. equities by aggressive foreign investors or changes in the size of cash balances held in large equity portfolios. The estimation of future price patterns in the equity market is a difficult and complex task, but given good projections of the individual variables, it is no harder than estimating future aggregate interest rates in the bond market. And supply/demand analysis for equities uses basically the same techniques that are used in interest rate forecasts—first the relatively independent factors of supply and the relatively independent factors of demand are estimated. Then the more changeable factors are studied individually to form a preliminary projection of total supply and total demand to see which way the market is likely to go—up or down—because some of the supply and demand factors will themselves be influenced by the trend of prices. For example, mutual fund sales will be higher in up markets than in down markets, while corporations will be more active in buying back their own stock in down markets. Gradually, using iterative analysis techniques, the analyst can refine his estimates into a coherent projection of the market price level that will bring supply and demand into equilibrium.

The basic strength of this approach is that it enables, even forces, the equity market strategist to think carefully about each component of supply or demand and then synthesize his analysis in a systematic way by estimating how each component may affect other components. On the other hand, this kind of analysis for both equities and bonds has one major weakness: these markets are always close to a long-term bal-

ance in supply and demand. Consequently, the margin for
error in forecasting either the stock or the bond market is not
very great, and so a strong change in just one or two major
factors can change the basic conclusion of the analysis. Consequently, a continuing surveillance should be maintained
so the strengths of this method of analysis will not be vitiated
by outdated information.

The purpose of supply/demand analysis is not, as one
might at first expect, to estimate actual prices of common
stocks or even of the leading stock market averages. Instead,
just as in supply/demand analysis in the bond market, the
purpose is to estimate not price, but the "capitalization" rate
—how much investors will pay for a stream of earnings in the
stock market or a stream of interest payments in the bond
market. In other words, supply/demand analysis aims at determining the probable direction and magnitude of change in
the P/E multiple.

The price earnings multiple is what investors pay for a
stream of common-stock earnings. Or, looked at the other
way around, the earnings/price ratio is what investors get in
earnings for their investment. And of course there are other
markets for other investments (bonds, land, mortgages, real
estate, oil royalties, venture capital, works of art, diamonds,
and so forth) which offer the investor returns on his investment. And each of these markets competes with every other
for the money of the marginal investor. So just as no stock is
really independent of any other stock, no market is really
independent of any other market. At least not for very long.

The "new era" approach to equities in 1967–68 argued
that the market price level was not a dependent variable, but
rather was the independently determined variable and that the
overall market P/E ratio was the dependent or subordinate
factor. To these optimists, P/E multiples had no independently determined value, but were just the pleats of the mar-

ket accordion, collapsing or expanding as necessary to make up the difference between changes in earnings (determined by corporate management's success) and changes in prices (determined by supply and demand). To make their point quite clear, assume for the moment that supply-and-demand factors would increase the equity market price level by 5 percent during a particular year. Now, if corporate earnings were to rise 10 percent in that year, the "new era" analysts argued that P/E multiples would be forced to *decline* by 5 percent to absorb the differential in rates of change. On the other hand, if instead corporate earnings were to decline by 10 percent in that year, then P/E multiples would *rise* by 15 percent to make up the differences. Obviously, this was a remarkably different way to try to understand the equity markets. The really wonderful part of their scheme was that demand was virtually always going to be greater than supply. So regardless of the year-to-year fluctuations in earnings, equity prices would always rise because demand would exceed supply. The whole idea was based on two assumptions. First, since institutional investors *had* been large and steady net buyers of common stocks, it was assumed that they would continue to be large net buyers of stocks (i.e., unlimited demand). Second, since corporations had not for many years been floating large new issues of common stock, it was assumed that they would not come to market very much in the future (i.e., limited supply). If both of these assumptions had in fact been valid, the stock market *would* have risen in perpetuity. But they weren't and it didn't.

The real point to be made is that simply projecting the pattern of the recent past is not an adequate substitute for developing a well-grounded understanding of what may change in the supply-demand equation and why it may change. For example, the utility and oil industries had become less liquid than usual by the end of the sixties and both industries had enormous capital investment programs ahead of them. At least part of the capital would come from large-scale sales of common stock—more than enough to overwhelm the margin by which past demand had exceeded past supply. So although supply/demand analysis is indeed a powerful tool, it must be used properly and carefully.

Supply/demand analysis is useful in projecting the trend of equity prices in general or the price of the equity market as a whole. It can also serve an important role in developing a profit maximizing strategy vis-à-vis the general equity market, and can help considerably in the selection of individual equities. For example, when price/earnings multiples are expected to expand, the bulk of that increase in P/E ratios will take place in the stocks showing superior relative earnings growth at that time.

One useful informal insight into the probable course of the equity market over the next 6 to 18 months is worth noting briefly. It is based on simply measuring the number and quality of new investment ideas coming from brokers who serve institutional investors. If the number and quality of "new purchase" recommendations is high and steadily rising, then the equity market can be characterized as a sellers' market and buyers will have to bid prices up to higher levels to "get a piece of the action." On the other hand, if there is a paucity of new ideas and new opportunities or a decline in the profit potential or profit assurance of "buy" recommendations, then prices will probably decline; and so caution would be in order. (This same "straws in the wind" method can be used to advantage in estimating which industries are overbought and likely to decline in price.)

While market analysis can make some useful contributions to long-term investment decisions, it more often concentrates on the trading decision. Trading decisions deal directly with the short-term price behavior of a security, and are usually made in terms of less than a month, and sometimes in minutes. At any one time, less than a dozen major institutions will be actively involved in either buying or selling a particular security. These institutions will largely determine the current price range and the volume of trading. (The specialist on the floor of the exchange and the individual or "retail" investor are usually followers and affect price only briefly and only slightly.) Other institutions that are interested in the stock as potential buyers or potential sellers can be brought into the active market either by changes in value due to new business developments or by significant changes in price. But within fairly wide price tolerances, they will be only latent sources of supply or demand, and the active participants in the market will be few. Consequently, the market analyst will try to determine how the active market participants in a stock are operating, and what the rough shape of their supply or demand schedules is so he can estimate the near-term probabilities for prices and transaction volume. At the same time, he attempts to evaluate how the inactive buyers and sellers might behave under various possible changes of circumstance.

The institutional trader, armed with regularly published statistical services that report the holdings and the changes in holdings of mutual funds and insurance companies, and actively pursuing his own "scuttlebutt research"—particularly contact with those few institutional brokers who are in frequent contact with all the major institutional investors in the United States, Canada, and Europe—can often determine how other institutions are or might become involved with various stocks and so anticipate near-term price by anticipating changes in active supply and active demand. How much is held by aggressive institutions? How large are their positions? At what prices did they buy? How has price and volume behaved recently? Do the holders "talk to each other" or do they act independently? Will the specialist help us to buy or sell? These are serious questions indeed. Since the costs of buying and selling large positions in a large portfolio are high—nearly 10 percent for a "round trip" according to the survey mentioned earlier—any success in reducing this cost could significantly increase annual portfolio profits for most institutional investors.

Market or price analysis also involves a longer term perspective that relates to months and years. There is, even among professional investors, a great tendency to focus attention on the present and near future. Market analysis can raise important questions that have a longer perspective, by directing attention to the current versus the long-term relative P/E multiple. (The P/E multiple of one stock or a group of stocks made *relative* to the P/E multiple of the S&P 500 Stock Index by dividing all stock multiples by the S&P multiple.)

As we discussed in Chapter 5, the relative price/earnings ratios of most well-established companies with relatively consistent historical patterns of earnings show a real consistency of staying within a normal range. As a consequence of this "normality," market analysis can identify price risk (historically high relative multiple which is likely to decline) and price opportunity (historically low relative multiple which is likely to rise to an average relative multiple). Although operating on the basis of relative multiples is not a sure path to large portfolio profits, this approach has been for many institutions a regular contributor to superior performance.

15

Analysis
and the portfolio

THE PURPOSE of this chapter is to close the loop of investment management by showing how analysis and portfolio activities interrelate in operational terms. The discussion is
pragmatic because while most investors agree on a high level
of abstraction that analysis and portfolio management should
work together, in all too many "real world" situations the
two functions are independent of or even antagonistic towards each other. Only by organizing to work effectively and
closely together can analysts and portfolio managers win for
their clients and for themselves the high profits that accrue
to objective and deliberate professional teamwork. Since
equity profits (and losses) can come from only two sources—
changes in per share earnings and changes in price/earnings
multiples—and since analysts specialize in the former while
portfolio managers specialize in the latter, a high degree of
positive cooperation can lead to profitable "cross fertiliza-
tion," just as surely as noncooperation will lead to "cross
sterilization." Strength in both areas is essential to sustained,

predictable, deliberate, superior performance with a large equity portfolio.

In general, simply because the analyst concerned with earnings is working in a quite different way and in a very different environment from the portfolio manager who is working with the market, they will probably find that the best way to cooperate is to let each "do his own thing." Obviously, this does not mean mutual avoidance. It simply means that each should be fully prepared to rely upon the other's expertise when that expertise suggests a particular decision should be made. They may properly ask each other searching questions, but analysts usually should not attempt to make market judgments and portfolio managers usually should not attempt to make earnings judgments.

This idea can be developed in terms of a simple pro-con matrix that is based on the analyst's judgment of earnings and the portfolio manager's judgment of P/E multiplier.

	"Pro" earnings	*"Con" earnings*
"Pro" multiplier	++	+−
"Con" multiplier	−+	−−

Ideally, only stocks that fall in the ++ category will be accepted. Unfortunately, this is not usually possible because there are not enough ++ stocks around, so +− stocks and −+ stocks will be accepted for portfolio use. It is in this uncertain, some-good-some-bad, world where cooperative effort is most needed. This is because the decision to buy or sell will depend not upon absolute judgments, but rather upon appraising the tradeoff between two very different variables which are understandable to only half of the decision-making team. Because questions of timing and market psychology are harder to explain logically and articulately, it is generally true that the portfolio manager has the last word in these "joint" decisions. This is probably sound if he acts only after being as sure as possible that he understands the nature of the negative or positive earnings judgment of the analyst. Since the portfolio manager is usually the final decision maker, the research objective is to develop and to transfer to him a valid understanding of the nature of the earnings of each company in whose stock he is operating.

Most investors believe the purpose of analysis is to obtain knowledge; they are wrong. Knowledge is always obsolescing. Too much time is required—of analysts and fund managers —to maintain current knowledge of the raw facts about stocks and companies. The real function of research is to develop a depth of *understanding* that will last for a relatively long period of time and will give the investment decision maker a valid frame of reference within which to appraise the significance of specific developments in the earnings of a company or the market behavior of its stock.

A realistic and useful understanding of the character of a company's earnings will involve an awareness of both positive and negative forces, all of varying degrees of importance, about which the analysts will have varying degrees of confidence. As in a huge skyscraper, some parts of the understanding will be structural while others will be functional and still others superficial. The architecture of a company's earnings can and should be sketched in a brief summary that will give the portfolio manager a convenient reference guide as to which factors are primary or secondary, which are based on internal or external factors, and how uncertain each is. Such summaries should be studied over and over again by the portfolio manager to avoid the risk of biasing the recollected description of earnings to accommodate changes in the market price. If he were operating only on market factors, the portfolio manager would be relying solely upon the superficial, generally available factors, and would probably have no competitive advantage vis-à-vis other skilled market operators.

In developing a superior understanding of present and potential portfolio holdings, the analysts are not dependent solely or even primarily upon the work they do themselves. They can and should develop a network of close working relationships with analysts at leading brokerage firms and at other investment management organizations. Their primary responsibility is not to invent profitable new ideas but to discover the best existing ideas (a role that is shared with portfolio managers for reasons explained in Chapter 2), and to develop, refine, and improve upon those ideas that can most enhance portfolio profits. The most profitable analysts will spend much of their time, energy, and imagination developing and managing a flow of information and judgments that will enable them to develop a superior understanding of earnings and so contribute significantly to portfolio profits.

In a very real sense, investment management organizations need to develop a group of analysis purchasing agents who would shop the various research organizations to obtain the best investment service values at the lowest commission cost. These men would not only manage the flow of information coming from brokers, but also manage the flow of commission compensation going back to the superior firms. This subject of "commission management" warrants further exploration.

Two factors have spurred brokerage investment services to institutional investors. First, a gap has developed between the direct cost of executing a large block order and the actual value of these block commissions to brokers. And second, the significance of this gap has increased as institutional commissions have multiplied both because managed assets grew substantially and because more aggressive management increased portfolio turnover. (Negotiated commissions will reduce, but not eliminate this "spread.")

The institutions' commissions and their demand for relevant services, have been powerful inducements which have drawn forth an impressive supply of professional investment services. In fact, so many firms now provide sophisticated research services tailored to institutional needs that the value to institutions of their commissions appears to have risen from a deep discount in the past to what can fairly be called a premium today.

The premium value of commissions can be seen in either of two ways. First, the services now provided by brokers would be far too costly for institutional investors to duplicate. For example, $1 million would hardly pay the salaries, travel, and overhead costs of a good in-house analytical staff of 20 people for a major institutional investor, but the same amount in commissions will buy the very best analytical efforts of five to ten superior research firms at no incremental cost beyond the commissions already resulting from regular changes in the portfolio.

Second, the value that can be added to the portfolio through effective use of broker-provided investment services far exceeds the dollar cost of commissions. Even an active portfolio with an 80 percent annual turnover rate would incur commission costs of less than one half of 1 percent of the total portfolio. Yet, an informal poll of aggressive institutional investors (conducted by the author) indicates that they believe brokerage research and advice add 3 to 5 percent to their portfolios' annual rate of return. Hence, the value added by broker research is several times the commission cost of acquiring these investment services.

This brings us back to the idea of commission management. The goal of commission management is to maximize the value received by the portfolio from judicious allocation of commission dollars. The first step toward effective research commission management is quite simple: take an inventory of the commissions controlled. What is the budget of commission buying power that can be spent on research and transaction services provided by brokers? The second step is to determine what services to buy. To make these decisions, and to develop a "shopping list," requires a thoughtful definition of the requirements of the portfolio management team.

Next, identify the strengths and weaknesses of the investment managers. They might ask themselves such questions as: What help can we use to maximize our investment strengths or minimize our investment weaknesses? Do we want economic analysis? Would discussions of portfolio strategy assist us? How about market timing? Do we need unusual liquidity to move large blocks quickly? How well do we really know the factors that determine the present and future earning power of all the companies in all the industries in which our portfolio already is or might be invested? How much do we need to know? Carefully thought out answers to these and other questions will provide the basis for determining what services to buy with a budget of commission dollars. The services should be those most useful to the particular portfolio management group and which cannot be developed independently either as well or as cheaply as they can be obtained from brokers. Easier said than done, it boils down to "know thyself."

In evaluating firms which are providing institutional investment services, commission managers will probably find a few firms that are unusually able to supply useful data, analysis, and judgments. Their approach to research is in tune with the needs of the portfolio managers. They have stimulating opinions, considerable amounts of valuable information, and an ability to assist in the development of appropriate portfolio strategy. Although their full range of services will probably be rather expensive because they are both costly to produce and highly valued by other institutional investors, the few firms in this group are the ones the commission manager will want to deal with most closely because their work can add the most to the portfolio.

Finding the commissions with which to acquire the best efforts of these superior firms may necessitate severing ties with other firms. This is often the toughest phase of implementing effective commission management, but it is also the most necessary. Based on his cost/benefit analysis, the commission manager will find several types of firms he can eliminate, just as the portfolio manager finds stocks he must sell to concentrate on better opportunities.

Many firms can probably be eliminated with no great loss in either breadth of coverage or depth of analysis, simply because there is a lot of duplication in research activities. Other firms have one or two people that are useful, but they may not be sufficiently better than the analysts in the basic research houses to warrant the commission cost of dealing with the whole firm. And some firms just don't happen to be providing the kind of services the portfolio really needs; while they may be fine services for others, they are unnecessary to the particular portfolio.

The basis of effective commission management is to maximize the service buying power of commissions by concentrating them intensively in a few very close working relationships. By concentrating commissions, the investment manager gains more time to do a better job with the firms he can really use well, and he gains more and better efforts from each of these firms. In brief, they will be better able to focus their efforts and provide the kind of counsel and information the portfolio manager can use most profitably. At the same time, the portfolio manager will become more fully familiar with all the research and evaluation that often does not appear in written reports: why specific securities are recommended; how heavily they should be weighted in the portfolio; which stocks look unattractive for purchase and which stocks should be considered for sale.

While managing commission outflows and brokerage research information inflows, the so-called "in-house" analysts should concentrate most of their time on understanding the stocks already in the portfolio—for many reasons. First, the stocks that are in the portfolio are clearly the stocks that will contribute the most to future portfolio profits or losses. Second, the profit or loss contributed to the portfolio's performance is not primarily a question of "was the stock owned?" but rather "was the stock a really large holding?" Weighting is really far more important than selection because a major holding will be four or five times as large and profit-powerful as a minor holding. Consequently, the analysts and the portfolio manager should always be concerned about the wisdom of increasing or decreasing the size of existing holdings. Working unusually skillfully with stocks they know best may well give the investment team a significant advantage over other investors who are less familiar with these stocks.

A third reason for concentrating research efforts on existing holdings is that most of the time and energy expended by most investment people is aimed at finding new stocks to buy. There is a substantial imbalance between the buying information system and the selling information system among professional investors. This is particularly true of the broker-analysts who are concerned that publishing a well-reasoned sale recommendation on one company will not just slam the door to that particular company's management, but will also lock doors at many other companies. The old saw "praise in public, criticize in private" has real meaning for the broker-analysts' work. In part because "buying information" is better

and more widely available, and in part because most investment managers are optimists, the selling decisions of institutional investors are generally inferior to their buying decisions. So if the analysts and fund manager concentrate on the
phase of portfolio management where the competition is
weakest, they can reasonably expect to gain a solid competitive advantage and so improve their relative portfolio performance.

Another, more subtle advantage gained from concentrating
on sale decisions is that by so doing, both the analyst and the
portfolio manager usually develop a clearer and stronger
definition of the key characteristics they want most to find in
any new stock purchase candidate. And also, they define
more clearly for themselves those particular features that they
want to avoid because their selling experience convinces them
that these features too often lead to losses or substandard
profits.

A fifth reason for concentrating on sale decisions is that
this work gives the only worthwhile basis for determining the
profit standards that should apply to all stocks in the portfolio
and to all stocks that might be considered for inclusion in the
fund. Each portfolio should have a minimum expected profit
requirement that is met by all stocks held. This minimum will
change as opportunities to buy superior new stocks wax and
wane, but it should always be known and should be rigorously
applied. The best way to set this hurdle rate of return is by
forcing yourself to weed out second rate performers and in
this way define the margin between good enough and *not* good
enough.

The final reasons for concentrating on existing holdings derives from simple mathematics. It would be unusual if more
than one out of five new purchase candidates were actually
purchased after careful research by the analyst. A more normal ratio might be one in ten. Assuming the analyst requires

two to three times as long to make an equally good judgment
on a new and unfamiliar stock as on an old and well-known
stock, the time invested in a single new purchase decision
can be 20 to 30 times as great as the time invested in making
a decision to increase significantly or greatly reduce one existing holding. Putting this ratio into the context of a large portfolio, the research on four or five new purchases might take
as long as a complete review of all the stocks already owned.
Since the real value of an investment decision is a direct function of the amount of capital and the potential profits that
are involved in executing that decision, the returns earned for
the portfolio by the analyst and the portfolio manager will be
greater if they concentrate on their largest opportunity—
managing the existing portfolio well.

Balancing the costs of research and prospective returns is
particularly difficult when an investment manager is considering purchase of a special group of stocks in small companies,
any one of which might enjoy spectacular growth in earnings
and share price appreciation in the future. The amount and
quality of analysis required to make superior investment decisions on very small companies is usually far too great to be
justified by the amount of capital that can be invested upon
each decision; the case must rest upon the actual profits to be
earned, not just the capital involved. The question boils down
to two parts: First, is available research time or available
portfolio capital the real constraint? And second, how profitable will a particular group of investors be working in this
highly specialized area? Realistic answers to the latter part of
the question would keep most institutional investment managers out of very small company investing.

Fortunately, this is not a "small or nothing" matter. Very
small stocks that appreciate (i.e., are successful) soon become leading candidates for the portfolio as regular investments. Indeed, those investors who have enjoyed the greatest

success with special small-company efforts maintain that the real profits (measured in dollars rather than in percentages) in their venture capital orientation actually come from knowing these small companies quite well when they become large enough to be made major investments. It is not clear that a special small-company effort is necessary, but it is clear that when the rare stocks are found, they should be used vigorously in the portfolio. If small-company investing leads to large positions in great stocks, it will pay off handsomely. Otherwise, it should be avoided. It all depends on the manager's investment philosophy.

Using great stocks vigorously does not require that they be major holdings *continuously*. Price is as important as value and even the shares of the very best companies can be overpriced at times. If the investment team is skilled at market operations, these shares should be sold when they are judged to be substantially overpriced. But, even when zero dollars are invested in it, the great stock should be analyzed just as carefully and as regularly as if it were a major holding simply because it probably will again be a major holding. This is important because superior portfolio profits can be earned by blending a merely average portfolio with a few major holdings in great stocks.

The major point of this chapter is that common stock profits can only come from changes in the EPS and the P/E, and the two subjects can and usually should be considered specialties. The investment manager who ignores one or the other or who confuses them in his operations is almost certainly going to underperform relative to the team that is strong in both areas and uses these strengths in tandem rather than at cross purposes. Most investment organizations tend, unhappily, toward the latter.

16

Selecting the investment manager

THE MOST IMPORTANT single decision that will be made by individual investors, endowment and pension trustees, and others concerned with and responsible for the long-term husbandry of capital is the selection of investment managers who are capable of successfully implementing a soundly conceived investment policy.

This is a difficult task in many ways. First, it seems "only natural" to many people to do the work of portfolio management themselves. It is fun; it is exciting. It is also very expensive!

Second, there is a very strong tendency for men and women who are entrusted with very large sums—particularly when they are so burdened for only a short term—to look for guidance to the most prestigious institutions with large pools of capital already under management, and to study the philosophy of capital preservation. But equity investment has more to do with growth than stability; it aims for capital productivity rather than capital preservation. The fully matured

174

financial organization is seldom capable of nurturing the creative environment needed for superior equity portfolio management.

Third, the most effective equity-oriented investment management organizations are often relatively new companies staffed largely by relatively young men and women. So the senior men and women who are responsible for selecting investment managers may well find themselves hard pressed to identify or identify with these superior management organizations. This problem is greatly compounded by the awkward fact that there is a continuing change in the front ranks of investment management that is not at all unlike the changes from year to year in the teams and the players at the top of big league sports. The increasing numbers of unusually bright and ambitious young men and women coming into the investment business promise to keep the leadership turnover relatively high. Consequently, the selection of investment managers is one decision that will not "stay decided" for very long. However, although the selection of investment managers is a difficult one, it is a critical decision that is being made either on purpose or by default for every large pool of capital. Too often, the decision is made by default. This chapter outlines one sensible approach to take for those who seek to make a sensible and intentional decision.

Investment management is a complex business that must be responsive to economic, social, cultural, political, and technological changes as well as to the continuing unfolding of business developments in major industries and individual companies, in addition to the day to day patterns in the capital markets. It is a demanding full-time job; and it is never a one-man show. Effective investment management requires simultaneous effectiveness in gathering relevant data, analyzing its meaning, synthesizing opportunities, and implementing timely actions. An effective investment manager is seldom an individual, but is rather a member of an organization that operates skillfully across the whole investment spectrum from business analysis through portfolio management to transactions in the capital market. Therefore, potential clients should make certain that all of these necessary skills are combined in any investment management candidate being considered.

Beyond these essential and fundamental capabilities, clients should analyze the system of incentives and rewards used within the organization to attract and motivate extraordinarily able men and women. Since an unusual degree of cooperation is required in this field to allow timely and accurate communication of often subtle insights, clients should look for openness; rigid lines of authority and internal competition usually are not helpful—they tend to restrict portfolio profits. Another important aspect of effective investment management is the financial control needed to keep accurate and up-to-date records of the holdings in the portfolio. Progressive portfolio management in today's turbulent and fast changing capital markets requires current records presented in convenient form. Quarterly reviews of 15-page portfolios lead almost inevitably to inferior results. Records that are inaccurate, tardy, or awkward can hurt portfolio performance since the portfolio manager who is uncertain of his position may not act confidently and in a timely manner.

Clients should also discuss with each prospective manager the way in which the portfolio will be managed with regard to such characteristics as number of holdings, reasons for changes, frequency of changes, maximum size of any one holding, and so on, to learn how their portfolio would actually be managed. Actual portfolios should be reviewed over a period of years to see how these investment practices were put into operation by each manager. In addition, clients should insist that the results of all managed funds be revealed; carefully selected "example" funds are too often chosen after the fact, and do not always show the average ability of the investment manager. (No client can really expect to achieve results that are above the manager's average.)

One final area of portfolio behavior should be considered specifically by the clients and the investment manager: the degree of volatility in market price that is acceptable. As discussed in earlier chapters, professional and academic studies have shown that over the long term, accepting higher volatility has lead to higher total returns for the portfolio. In other words, if you can tolerate the vibrations, you can get higher long-term portfolio profits. On the other hand, we have identified the concept of Utility that says that beyond some point, higher profits may not be worth the concurrently higher volatility of the portfolio in the view of the client. So to avoid unnecessary future misunderstanding, clients should review this area carefully with specific reference to how the manager's portfolios have behaved in the past, relative to the market, in regard to both volatility and rate of return. In brief, the client should be confident that a prospective investment management organization has investment objectives comparable to those the client himself has for the fund. Since investment management organizations typically specialize in a particular approach to fund management, clients will probably find that they are seeking a combination of organizational philosophy and competence that is congruent with their own long-term financial objectives.

Clients should consider the total size of capital managed by the prospective investment manager. In today's capital market environment, it appears that investment organizations responsible for very large sums experience inefficiencies of operation that retard portfolio performance appreciably. Over the years, as the markets have become more liquid, larger and larger pools of capital have been able to operate smoothly, and it seems highly probable that the expansion of

liquidity will continue, but at present the upper limit on effi-
cient management of progressive portfolios appears to be
about $2 billion. Clients seeking high total returns should, in
general, seek smaller organizations.

Another important consideration involving the size of the
total capital managed is the practical desirability of being an
important customer to the manager. In very large investment
organizations, even a portfolio of $10 million will not seem
important and as a result may get less than the best the manager can offer. This is neither appropriate nor necessary. A
portfolio of this size can readily find an investment manager
of superior skill for whom such a portfolio would clearly be
an important client. (Smaller funds—under $1 million—
should recognize that the best managers will not be greatly
interested in having their account for separate management,
and should instead join with other smaller funds in special
mutual funds developed for the very purpose of providing
"best client" services to smaller portfolios.)

While no client should put himself in the unrewarding position of being a small, not very important account, neither
should a client put himself in the position of being too big and
too important. For example, if an investment manager's present clients are generally between $5 and $30 million, it
would be most unwise to become the only $100 million client
for several reasons. First, the organization and the individual
manager are not accustomed to operating a portfolio of that
size. Second, that account is axiomatically too important to
lose to the investment management company and therefore to
the individual portfolio manager. His associates will all be
too tempted to "look over his shoulder." He will be ill at
ease with the client and will tend to avoid those tentative con-
victions on selection and strategy that are typically the most
profitable, and emphasize the surer things—a tendency that
does not lead to profit maximization in an equity portfolio.

A practice which is quite widely used in the pension fund field, and is now gaining broader acceptance among other clients because it offers several advantages to the very large client, is the concept of diversifying a portfolio by dividing it among several investment managers, that is, "diversification by manager." Larger clients can benefit in several ways by dividing their total assets among two, four, or even more different investment management organizations. First the individual managers will be motivated by competition with other managers, and regular reapportionments of the capital can reinforce this factor, so the client will get "best customer" efforts from each and every manager. In addition, the client will have an appropriate guide for reviewing the managers' results by comparing them to each other; it will be very clear if one manager or another is not pulling his oar! The most important advantage is that among aggressive managers investment styles differ appreciably and individual managers have "hot" and "cold" periods during different phases of different markets, but a portfolio that is diversified among several managers will, in aggregate, experience the highly desirable average results of several expert managers while avoiding the acute distress of having only one manager who happens to be temporarily "out of tune" with a particular market phase. Thus, diversification by management can be helpfully encouraging to clients who seek to change to more aggressive management for the equity capital for which they are responsible, but are frankly uncertain as to how to pick *the one best manager.*

Diversification by management can be achieved either vertically or horizontally. Some clients may wish to divide the total fund into separate subfunds each of which will have a different investment mission such as (*a*) highly liquid reserves, (*b*) long-term bonds, (*c*) emerging growth stocks, (*d*) blue-chip stocks, (*e*) oil royalties, and (*f*) real estate. In such a case, different managers would probably be selected for each subfund. This is vertical diversification. Horizontal diversification would involve dividing the total fund among several investment managers with all having the same investment mission, but with the knowledge that they would each seek to achieve that same goal in their own different ways.

Although some clients have obtained good results with so-called in-house portfolio managers, this approach usually is not successful because it is too costly and too difficult to reproduce, for a single client, a full-fledged investment management organization that can compete successfully with the best independent organizations. On the other hand, a strong financial man who can guide the preparation of long-range financial plans and review the investment results of the independent portfolio managers is a most valuable asset to any client organization. He can act as the professional buyer of professional investment services. It would seem folly to expect this valuable and probably overextended financial manager to run the portfolio too. He probably could not do it well, and his other responsibilities are too important to be slighted.

Selecting the investment manager to implement a well-developed investment policy is not a terminal decision. The managers must be managed. So long as substantial sums of equity capital are entrusted to professional managers, clients must be regularly concerned with the measurement and review of portfolio operations to be sure that the portfolio managers are achieving the intended results. This very important responsibility should be carried out with care and regularity. Ideally, the portfolio will be organized on the "unit of account" basis, developed by the mutual funds, in which the whole portfolio is divided into "shares" of rather small sums (typically about $10) and the investment performance is then measured in per unit terms. This technique has a subtle but powerful total advantage; it concentrates on measuring results of the portfolio and avoids the distractions of reviewing individual securities which so often defy accurate evaluation. The "unit of account" also offers a most convenient way to review quantitative results; its very convenience is an important inducement to the clients to measure and review portfolio results regularly.

The investment performance of the portfolio should be compared regularly with leading mutual funds, market averages, and with other comparable portfolios because the client needs to have reliable measures of the ability of the investment managers to achieve superior results relative to the market and relative to the results achieved by other managers with funds having comparable goals.

In addition to a quantitative check on results which may be made monthly, the investment committee of any large institutional client should hold review meetings with the investment managers at least once each year and preferably once each quarter. These meetings should not concentrate on results achieved, but rather on how and why these results were accomplished. The managers' expectations for the next several months should be presented to the clients during these meetings together with a well-reasoned portfolio strategy to capitalize on these expectations. In other words, the client should act toward the portfolio managers in much the same way a board of directors would act toward operating management in a business corporation.

Review of investment operations over a period of years may oblige a client to discharge the inadequate manager. If called for, this action should be taken promptly because no client should long endure less than the best investment management. In general, clients should allow an investment manager to demonstrate his abilities over a full market cycle simply because some managers excel in bull markets while others succeed in bear markets. However, if the investment manager or his organization has undergone a significant structural change (such as a change in ownership, senior management, or the like), the consequences of the change should be probed quite carefully to be certain they will not be adverse to the client's interests. Failure to follow agreed policy faithfully is, of course, grounds for immediate dismissal of the manager.

On a more positive note, the client should have and demonstrate real consideration for his investment manager. Clients will usually be surprised how much benefit they will gain from showing interest in and enthusiasm for their investment managers. (Any competitor does better when he has a strong and partisan cheering section.)

Clients should anticipate two requirements commonly made by the more successful managers. The first is full discretion in portfolio operations. The benefits of providing such discretion are obvious: the manager can act as soon as he decides on a course of action rather than going through the often cumbersome motions of obtaining consent from the client before implementing the investment decision. The delays incurred in obtaining client approvals can be expensive in three ways: sales may be made too late; purchases may be made too late; and some actions may never even be proposed. This latter cost is probably greatest because frankly the best actions are often the hardest to explain logically. The manager who requires discretion is ready to accept full responsibility for his influence on the portfolio rather than trying to dilute his role by having consultations with others. This acceptance of responsibility is important; the requisite authority should go with it. In point of fact, any investment manager who does not insist on discretion should probably be avoided.

Although study of the relevant law clearly shows that endowment and pension trustees may delegate the authority to manage a portfolio on a day-to-day basis, some may be concerned about the resulting loss of control. A simple but effective resolution of this problem is to have notice of transactions sent to the client who can then raise questions if he sees fit so to do. If it is deemed necessary, then the client can exercise a veto and request reversal of any "offending" individual transaction. The notification can be made within a few days of each individual transaction so a reversal can be made in less than a week if necessary. (This is the so-called Harvard System because of its origin: the veto power has never been actually exercised by the trustees of Harvard University.) This simple procedure can be usefully reassuring to clients who are shifting from conservative to progressive methods of portfolio management.

Second, the more successful investment managers charge what may at first appear to be high fees for their services. Clients who seek a progressive management rather than custodial services should be encouraged to accept these fees because without high incomes, the investment management organizations could not attract and motivate the skilled managers needed for successful portfolio management. On the other hand, with these skilled managers, higher total returns earned by the portfolio should repay the fees many times over. Portfolio management is uniquely a "people business," and investments in obtaining superior management usually return noticeably superior investment results.

Clients engaged in selecting professional investment managers must be keenly aware that they are engaged in making an extraordinary investment decision, the long-term consequences of which can be far greater than any other financial decision they will make. They should devote the requisite time and care to making this crucial judgment. Perhaps the greater challenge is to take what may seem a bold initiative, reaching past the managers who are reported generally to be the best to find the managers who really are the best. As Yale's great Dean William C. Devane advised: "Be bold, be bold . . . but not too bold."

17

The endowment fund
as client

THE STRENGTH and quality of many of our country's most important cultural, educational, and philanthropic institutions depend on the funds that they draw from their endowments. But, because of sustained cost escalation and insufficient endowment income, these vital national institutions are now confronting a financial crisis that is already serious and is rapidly getting worse.

One analysis of the needs and resources of 20 apparently well-endowed colleges and universities concluded that by 1978 they would be running a combined annual deficit of more than $100 million. Several universities, including Yale, Columbia, Princeton, and Cornell (which all have relatively large endowments) have already reported deficits. Other universities have avoided "losses" by postponing highly desirable projects; but this is only replacing "financial deficit" with an even more serious "education deficit." And other types of endowed institutions, such as hospitals, museums, schools, churches, libraries, and companies of performing artists, are

185

suffering from similar problems. Ironically, because we have learned to expect so much more each year from these institutions, their very success may be their financial undoing. Unless vigorous, constructive action is taken soon, the financial strains that lie ahead for almost all privately financed institutions will be disruptive, and could be destructive.

To help trustees fulfill their mission more effectively, this chapter first defines the nature of the financial problem facing privately endowed institutions and then proposes a practical, systematic approach toward a sound solution. However, it should be clearly recognized that the proposed solution (or any other solution) can be put to work only by individual trustees at individual institutions.

The basic financial problem for almost all endowed institutions is that costs have risen more rapidly than revenues. In other sections of the economy, labor-saving equipment has substantially increased the productivity of workers. But in activities such as education, medicine, the performing arts, and museums, the two dominant costs are salaries and facilities; and for these factors of production, only modest productivity gains have been possible, while their costs have risen more rapidly than have most other kinds of costs. Thus, the cost per unit of output has been rising much faster than the national average rate of inflation. The result has been severe financial strain. Although many steps have been taken to meet these escalating costs, with some success so far, the future does not look encouraging. Many of the resources which have been called on in the past cannot be expected to be adequate for the future's continuously growing needs.

The endowed institutions have vigorously cultivated their external sources of funds. From the private sector, important infusions of money have come from expanded fund-raising programs which often are conducted with an effective combination of amateur vigor and professional precision. But even the professional fund raisers are unwilling to predict that future gains will keep pace with those of the past. Tuitions and fees have been increased rapidly, but further increases at comparable rates could make the services of these institutions prohibitive in price unless some form of outside subsidy is forthcoming. Government support has increased substantially since World War II, but further increases in government funding could pose philosophical and public policy questions about excessive government influence on private institutions.

While these external sources have carried much of the increased financing burden thus far, the main internal source of funds—the general endowment—has lagged, and typically it has lagged badly. Since 1940, although absolute income from endowments has grown, their contribution to the total income of institutions has fallen sharply—from 46.8 percent to 13.4 percent for one group of private colleges and universities. And general surveys indicate that the decline for other kinds of institutions has been comparable. The failure of endowment support to keep pace with the spending obligations of our nation's private institutions has resulted in a financial squeeze that has already become acute and promises to become severely disruptive unless changes are made soon. Looking to the endowment funds as an opportunity to catch up with rising costs makes sense.

The main reason behind the lagging contribution from endowments is that most of the large endowments were established and funded before World War II, and during the past 25 years new additions to private endowments have been comparatively modest. Without major new sources of capital, the growth of most endowments must be achieved with existing capital. They have had to produce their own growth. Yet, the growth of endowments has not kept pace with that of mutual funds and other large investment portfolios. (If endowments had achieved even average results, the present problem would be greatly reduced.) Unfortunately, however, as endowment capital growth has lagged, so too has endowment income lagged. And so endowment investments have been neither as profitable as they need to be nor as profitable as they could be.

Why hasn't this problem been solved? The reasons for general inaction and passivity in endowment management are important to understand; the most powerful restraint appears to be an organizational one. Quite candidly, most trustees simply do not understand the "nitty gritty," "day-to-day," "real world" work of the hospital, museum, dance company, university, or foundation that has invited them to serve. (And they would be the first to say so. The invitation to serve is a civic honor that is hard to turn down.) Trustees, well intentioned as they usually are, often are quite unfamiliar with the operations, budgeting, and spending of the institution. So these "operating finances" or expenditures are usually left entirely to the administration. On the other hand, the responsibility for income is divided into three parts. The administration is responsible for setting fees for admission, membership, tuition, and so forth. The administration divides with trustees the responsibility for fund raising. And the trustees, usually without a clear knowledge of the current financial position or the financial future of the institutions they are striving to serve, are given full responsibility for the endowment. (After all, they're financial people. And besides, what else can they do?)

Unhappily, the result of this division of responsibility is that the main areas of fiscal management are separated, and their separate management leads to conflicting objectives which can quickly raise such critical questions as the following. Should the proposed new medical school be launched when the endowment is already strapped for income? Should fees be raised even more or should more funds be expended from the endowment? Should income from fund raising be spent entirely on current programs or should some be invested in the endowment to help finance future programs? Etcetera? Etcetera? This divided responsibility for fiscal affairs leads naturally and directly to inaction. And problems as serious as those faced by endowed institutions are not overcome by inaction.

What should be done? The first and most important step is for trustees to actively involve themselves in the fiscal affairs of the institutions they seek to serve. They should insist upon the following:

1) Clear statements of the institution's objectives together with priority rankings among major programs.

2) Cost/benefit analysis of major programs to support the above priorities.

3) Projections of future income by source (fees, contributions, government contracts, endowment, and so on) and projections of future expenses by program and activity. The projections should be made for periods of at least five years into the future to provide suitable lead times for planning and remedial reaction to adverse experience as and if it unfolds. These projections should be supported by frequent and regular reviews with explicit comparisons of budgets with actual experience, just as would be expected in any well-managed business organization.

4) Regular studies of such nonprogram support services as food, laundry, maintenance, custodial, and so on, to determine whether costs can be reduced in these areas.

5) Effective management of endowment capital, the focus of this book.

Beyond these basic requirements, trustees should move towards a *systems* concept of the financial circumstances of the institutions they serve. The above-mentioned requirements are important to the sound development of the components of financial management, but the really important, value-adding efforts will take these components and integrate them into a systematic conceptualization of the financial dynamics of the institution as a whole. With a systems concept of finances, trustees and administrators can turn usefully to crucial *policy* issues. They can determine appropriate tradeoffs such as the choice between higher present spending on current programs versus building up endowment capital from which to draw higher income for program funding in future years; the choice between emphasis on graduate student programs versus undergraduate education in a university; the choice between a new painting or a new education program in an art museum; or the choice between new equipment or new staff for a hospital. The essential point is that a clear financial understanding enables trustees to probe the critical policy issues of spending for institutional purposes as well as to offer their business management expertise to cost reduction in existing programs. Effective financial analysis will help trustees become useful and creative participants in the life and purpose of the institution because even for the most eleemosynary institution, money matters greatly, and astute fiscal management can be of critical importance to the vitality and scope of any institution's program.

Perhaps the most valuable result of a systems analysis of an institution's finances will be a clearer focus on the opportunity and the need to make endowment capital more productive; to make it catch up to the need for increasing spendable funds; to use endowment capital not as an insurance reserve, but as the vital equity capital of the institution; to make the endowment fundamentally progressive and oriented to achievement rather than defensive and passive as has been the case all too often in the past.

Since most readers are probably already quite familiar with the operating and budgeting requirements of effective business management, and since fund raising is a specialized field that warrants separate discussion, the remainder of this chapter concentrates on the endowment fund and its potential role in the overall financial system of the institution by discussing what can be done for and with an endowment to make its capital more fully productive in the service of the institution to which it belongs.

The first step in making an endowment more productive for its institution is to recognize that the long-term nature of privately endowed institutions demands an equally long-term perspective for endowment fund management. The "long term" for a university may well be *perpetuity*. In contrast, five years has often been called "infinity" by professional investors. An endowment investment committee will usually experience real difficulty in trying to develop an investment program in step with the long-term financial needs of an institution if it also tries to keep pace with the faster rhythms of the capital markets. The two have incompatible, contradictory tempos. Therefore, trustees should divide their investment responsibilities into two parts: long-range policy decisions and current period portfolio operations. Then the investment committee can concern itself primarily with major policy considerations and delegate day-to-day operation of the endowment portfolio to full-time investment managers.

Unfortunately, most endowment investment committees tend to define their task in terms of buying and selling individual stocks or bonds. This approach is usually wrong for two reasons:

1) Since committees are notoriously unsuccessful at making effective decisions, and since complex investments cannot be well managed in two-hour sessions held once every three months, most investment committees do not make good portfolio operating decisions.

2) Such detailed activity will distract committee members from their really important mission, which is to set policy goals and review portfolio operations to ensure that they are consistent with the trustees' long-term objectives. Not only are *policy* decisions more important than *operating* decisions, but they also make better use of the experienced judgment that trustees are expected to bring to an institution.

The major policy areas for a well-managed endowment fund include the following:

• What funds should be made available for current spending versus reinvestment for future capital growth?
• What degree of liquidity should be maintained?
• What investment characteristics (e.g., quality, diversification, volatility, and turnover) are necessary or desirable?
• How should the investment manager be selected?
• How can the investment committee work with the manager so as to keep portfolio operations in accord with investment policy?

These are difficult and challenging questions. If they are resolved wisely, the results can be highly beneficial to the endowment and the institution it serves. In the remaining sections of this chapter we explore some answers to these questions.

Spending is the critical frontier at which the endowment should interface constructively with the programs and purposes of the institution. Unfortunately, most endowment funds are run without special regard for the specific needs and opportunities of the institutions they are intended to support. Nowhere is this more apparent than in deciding what funds are made available for current spending. For many years, and for most institutions, this decision was made in a standard, but arbitrary manner: income received as dividends, rent, and interest was "spendable now," but nothing more or less than this "income"was to be spent on current activities.

The simplicity of this decision rule is deceptive. It is potentially dangerous because it puts unnecessary emphasis on current "cash income" and therefore leads typically to an undue quest for investments with unusually large current yields rather than seeking investments that offer a suitable balance between current returns and the capacity for future growth in capital from which will come higher future yields. Specifically, an overemphasis on present yields usually means a portfolio concentration on bonds, which offer little or no prospect of capital growth, or on equities of mature corporations with limited and uncertain prospects for growth. But without long-term growth in capital, an institution's steadily rising need for spendable funds will inevitably outstrip the ability of the endowment fund to meet its share of budget needs. Such a policy is neither wise nor necessary.

It is true that in trust law the antagonistic interests of the income beneficiary and the remainderman are conveniently and reasonably resolved by sharply separating income from capital. But, as Professor William Cary has eloquently and rigorously demonstrated, endowments are subject not to trust law, but rather, to corporate law, in which profits from operating "income" and profits from "gain" in capital values are considered equivalent and should be treated as equals. (W. L. Cary and C. B. Bright, *The Law and the Lore of Endowment Funds,* Ford Foundation, 1969.) As Cary points

out, endowment trustees are not obligated to accept the rule
that "only cash income is spendable." They can, and should,
determine the best division of all investment profits between
present and future spending for each particular institution.

It is interesting at this point to recall the "prudent man
rule" which is so often used to "justify" the traditional approach, because a modern interpretation would probably
bring its meaning into accord with the implications of Cary's
analysis. This "rule" was defined by Justice Samuel Putnam
in an 1830 decision as follows:

All that can be required of a trustee is that he shall conduct himself faithfully and exercise a sound discretion. He is to observe
how men of prudence, discretion, and intelligence manage their
own affairs, not in regard to speculation, but in regard to the
permanent disposition of their funds.

Today, the men to whom Justice Putnam referred generally
follow a policy of seeking high total returns on investments
and do not make an artificial distinction between income and
gains. These "prudent men" recognize that dividends, rents,
interest, and capital appreciation are all forms of investment
profit, and that the objective of their investment programs is
a sustained, high rate of total profits from a combination of
all these sources. This deliberate pursuit of investment profits
from all sources is often called the Total Return Concept.

The essence of the Total Return Concept is this: in considering overall investment profit, the *amount* is more important
than the *form* in which profits are earned—that is, a dollar
of capital gain is exactly equal to a dollar of income. Not
only has the total return objective won general acceptance
among large individual investors, but it is also being applied increasingly to corporate pension funds and endowment
funds, both of which are exempt from the distortions of personal income tax rates. The Total Return Concept is also

responsive to the nature of equity investment in our contemporary business economy. Business managers are reinvesting large amounts of retained earnings to provide future growth; as a result, more equity investment profits are being earned in the form of capital gains than as dividends.

Adoption of the total return approach frees the investment manager from the artificial constraints of trust law, thus allowing him to seek the highest profits from all sources, which in turn allows the trustees to decide for themselves how to divide the total returns between present and future spending to suit the particular needs of the particular institution.

When an investment committee wisely rejects the simplistic division of "income" and "gain" profits, it must make two important decisions:

- What is a realistic Total Return objective?
- How should the returns be divided between current spending and reinvestment for capital growth to support future spending?

Rejecting the arbitrary rule that dividends, interest, and rents will be spent currently, trustees implicitly accept the responsibility to find a wiser basis for dividing total returns between present needs and future needs. They should establish a prudent discipline to guide current spending from the endowments. A formal Spending Rule should be developed partly to avoid future misunderstandings and partly to assure that careful reasoning has gone into the determination of the rule. The main objective of spending rules is to establish a prudent discipline that balances present money demands and future needs. The upper limit on spending should be set so as to provide for the maintenance of the capital base, and this should be done in terms of purchasing power rather than nominal dollar figures. That is, part of the total return should be reinvested to offset the erosion of inflation. For example:

If the trustees decide that a 10 percent annual total return (yield plus capital gain) is a realistic long-run average expectation, and if a 2.5 percent rate of inflation is assumed, then the maximum amount available for current spending, after providing for maintenance of the capital base, would be 7.5 percent of the original capital base. The remaining 2.5 percent of total return would automatically be reinvested in the fund to maintain its purchasing power. Beyond this basic approach to the true preservation of capital, and in view of rising costs of programs for the institution, the trustees may well wish to provide for further capital growth by adopting an even higher retention rate. These are difficult decisions that must balance future needs and sources of income with present needs. That is, the decisions involve institutional philosophy as well as investment opportunity.

In determining the spending level, trustees must be careful not to assume a rate of total return that may not be achievable. One way to protect against this is to make no assumption at all about probable future returns but, rather, to work from actual results achieved over the past several years, or a specific fraction of these actual average returns. A moving-average total return guideline has the advantage of being demonstrably realistic, and of adjusting automatically to changes in the return realized by the endowment fund. In addition, a multiyear time frame encourages everyone to think more carefully of the long-term financial needs of the endowment and the institution to which it must always be responsive. Actually, the specific details of the spending rule are less important than a clear recognition by the trustees that the division of the total investment return is a matter of *choice*, and that active, conscious choice is a vital investment policy that can add importantly to the contribution the endowment makes to its institution.

Another major policy question facing the trustees is how

much liquidity is required in the endowment fund and the best way of ensuring that this liquidity will be available when it is needed. Liquidity is important mainly during periods of financial adversity, so this decision involves consideration of the defensive posture that will be taken to protect the institution from disruption due to a temporary, but perhaps severe, financial squeeze, such as might arise during a prolonged recession. In most endowment funds, the liquidity policy manifests itself in a major, often dominating, position in bonds, typically between 40 percent and 60 percent of the whole portfolio. Many people believe a large position in bonds was made obligatory by the prudent man decision cited earlier, but this view is not correct. Modern "prudent men" usually do not own bonds. A more important reason for minimizing bond holdings is that bond investments seldom pass the requirements of total return objectives because they offer no real growth in capital (as discussed in Chapter 3). So fixed-income investments should be kept to a minimum and used only to meet emergency liquidity needs.

From a policy viewpoint, an important problem with the traditional bond/stock ratios in endowment portfolios is that they are established as though the portfolio were a static entity, whereas it should be viewed as a dynamic contributor to the institution's ongoing program. Therefore, the determination of a proper defensive reserve of fixed-income securities should be made from a funds flow analysis rather than from balance sheet ratios. A careful analysis of flow of funds will usually lead to assigning the defensive role to a small, specialized part of the portfolio. The rest of the fund is then available for Total Return investments. The defensive reserve can provide the institution with precious protection from economic adversity, but the more important advantage of this practice is that it protects the endowment from excessive emphasis on a too-general defense against uncertainty or adversity and allows a progressive, profit-maximizing approach to the management of most of the funds. Thus, even assuming a five-year period of economic adversity during which dividend and interest income is cut by 50 percent—assumptions that describe a severe depression—a reasonable total defensive reserve would probably be less than 15 percent of the total fund. This small but sufficient reserve contrasts sharply with the large bond positions so common to endowments. The critical element in this approach is acceptance of the principle that, if necessary, the entire defensive reserve is wholly expendable during a crisis to maintain the endowment's contribution to current operations. Of course, this commitment to spend as necessary must be balanced by a policy of regular contributions to build up the reserve in more prosperous periods. The relatively small defensive reserve is the *only* part of the entire fund which is necessarily invested in fixed income securities. As a result of carefully analyzing the flow-of-funds reserve requirements, defensive responsibilities can be assigned to this small, specialized part of the portfolio rather than imposing an unnecessarily general burden on the whole portfolio. All of the rest of the fund would then be available for total return investment.

Another advantage of the defensive reserve is that by assuring that liquidity needs will be met effectively, the trustees will feel less pressure to limit equity investments to presumably "safe" stocks of mature companies in mature industries which historically earn lower total returns than do less mature, but more rapidly growing companies. In considering both equities and bonds, the small specialized defensive reserve frees trustees from traditionally vague and generalized defensive positions and allows them to commit most of the endowment capital to the pursuit of high total returns, the proper primary objective for the fund.

Another possible policy question for trustees is the mix of such portfolio characteristics as the maximum or minimum number of individual issues, the maximum size for any single holding, limits on turnover within the portfolio, and the "quality" of the investments. These rules will be at best awkward efforts to define the characteristics the trustees find suited to their total return objectives. At worst, they can be real constraints on the operating investment manager and will limit the total return he should be able to attain. Trustees should develop these guidelines in cooperation with their investment managers, and avoid setting unnecessarily confining rules. To avoid future misunderstandings, the trustees should review carefully with the investment manager how his portfolios have behaved in the past and what degree of volatility will be acceptable to the institution. If the managers have been wisely chosen, and if they understand the investment objectives, strict operating rules are not needed; rather, by hampering the managers, they are likely to do more harm than good.

In concluding this chapter, it seems proper to restate the problem. Private educational, cultural, religious, medical, and philanthropic institutions which have contributed so greatly to the quality of our national way of life are facing a severe financial crisis that is at least partly due to the failure of endowment funds to keep pace with either the needs of these institutions or the opportunities in the capital markets. A major change is needed. Some trustees have already initiated programs to reorganize and redirect endowment fund management and to integrate endowment operations with the program operations of the institution. This chapter has drawn upon the experience of several of these innovators to present a broad program that can be adopted by the leaders of almost any endowed institution. The guidelines presented here have all been tested and proven useful, but the ultimate test of their value is whether they are adapted to the specific needs and opportunities of individual institutions, and this in turn is a matter only the trustees can determine.

18

The pension fund as client

Pension funds are the biggest, fastest growing, fast changing aggregation of private capital in the United States today. Taking employee benefit plans as a whole—including corporate pension funds for salaried and hourly employees; profit sharing, thrift, and savings plans; pension funds of municipal, county, and state employees; and funds for teacher retirements and union funds—the total assets were nearly $200 billion by 1971.

Yet, surprisingly little has been written about the proper strategic approach that should be taken towards the management of these enormous assets. In part, this is an understandable result of the phenomenal growth of these assets, but now the time has come to pull together the best thinking that has developed in this field and to propose a basic framework for developing and implementing an overall strategy for managing the assets committed to supporting pension programs. Corporate pension funds, the neglected giants of corporate financial management, may well be heading into a crisis unless top management moves promptly to make long-term financial planning for pension funds an important function.

Judging from recent surveys of pension management policies and practices in large corporations by Louis Harris and Associates, here is one way to summarize the problem: although pension funding contributions and benefit payments have been rising at nearly 15 percent, compounded annually, and even though most executives interviewed expect this rate to continue or even increase because of inflation, vesting, portability, parity pensions, and early retirement, these executives somehow do not expect their own companies' contributions or benefits to rise as much as 5 percent over the next five years. Now, it would be impossible for the *average* company's fund obligation to rise at a 15 percent rate if all the *individual* company obligations rose by only 3 to 5 percent *unless* the actuarial rate-of-return assumption were increased to make up the difference. And this is what many companies have been doing: the assumed rates of return on pension portfolio investments have gone from 3.5 percent to 5.0 percent on average. Further proportionate increases in the assumed rate of return (to more than 7 percent compounded annually) will be harder and harder to justify on the basis of actual investment results. So when the slack provided by the formerly low actuarial assumption gets used up, the growth in pension obligations will have to be met by real money, not by accounting adjustments.

Many corporations are not preparing themselves for this potentially abrupt change; the survey found that a substantial majority of the senior executives responsible for pension funds spend only a small portion of their time on pension policy and make no long-term forecasts of either future benefits or of the future contributions that their companies will have to pay into their funds.

The consequences of inadequate preparedness could be

seriously disruptive to the corporation, to pension beneficiaries, and to management. So we need strategic planning for pension funds now because these funds are so large. Consider these facts:

- The largest corporate pension fund has assets of nearly $9 billion, whereas the largest mutual fund has assets of less than $2.5 billion.
- Total corporate pension assets are more than $125 billion; more than the combined 1970 net assets of General Motors, Standard Oil, Ford, General Electric, IBM, Chrysler, Mobil, Texaco, ITT, Gulf Oil, Western Electric, and U.S. Steel.
- In 1970, more than $15 billion went into pension funds, about the same amount by which total bank credit increases in this country in a typical year.
- By 1980, annual corporate pension contributions are expected to reach $25 billion, an amount equal to 1970's total dividends paid to stockholders.
- Pension funds for state, county, and municipal retirement systems are growing even faster than private funds. And they already add up to $55 billion in assets.

This chapter takes the view that the effective management of pension funds depends upon the joint determination by investment managers and pension executives of a sound, long-range strategy for the deployment and use of these enormous assets. On the other hand, such significant tactical subjects as actuarial projections, integration with social security programs, and the like, are not covered here. In point of fact, these complex tactical questions have attracted so much attention in recent years that they have distracted investment managers and pension executives from concentrating on the long-range strategic questions which now must be put into focus. This latter task is the ambitious purpose of this chapter.

The private corporate pension fund is really only one of several types of employee benefit plans, so before exploring their optimum strategy as clients of investment managers, a few notes on other types of benefit programs are appropriate. Public pension funds for state, county, and city employees, or for teachers' retirement are often restricted in the range of investment alternatives that are allowed, and in the degree to which particular investment media can be emphasized, by state and local laws. Since this is a highly technical, often arcane area, and because many of the self-imposed restrictions are now being removed, these problems will be ignored here. Still, it is worth noting that these assets are intended to serve the same basic purpose as the private corporate pension funds and, except for local governmental restrictions, should be managed in essentially the same manner. (Most of the existing local government regulations should be removed.)

Profit sharing plans, savings plans, and thrift plans are also tax exempt employee benefit plans that are often lumped together with pension plans, but they are very different in important ways and so should be treated quite differently in terms of investment policy and objectives. The principal difference is that in these plans the individual participant experiences quite directly the full consequences of the day-to-day investment results of the investment portfolio. Such is not the case with a pension fund. This difference is critical.

It can be fairly advocated that with the typical pension fund, the corporation and the employees share the benefits of superior investment performance because if the pension "pie" is greatly enlarged due to superior investment results, the company may well share some of this "surplus" with employees by increasing their total pay or fringe benefits. On the other hand, the company would bear all of the costs of adverse performance because the corporation has to make up any untoward investment losses. In the profit sharing plan, however, the individual employee has what amounts to a personal investment account with the manager of the plan and will experience quite directly the gains and losses of the fund both over the long term and in the short run.

This difference can become abruptly clear when the individual employee retires. Regardless of market fluctuations and regardless of investment achievements, the pension fund will pay precisely—not more and not less than—the amount the company and the retiring employee have expected all along. But, the profit sharing plan payout may be either a lot higher *or* a lot lower than indicated even by reports of investment results the employee has received in the recent past. Harshly adverse stock market experience can suck the expected positive rewards and incentives right out of such a plan, and a sudden change in expectations can be especially distressing to retiring employees. So before returning to the major subject of this chapter, the corporate pension fund, the investment policy implications of the special characteristics of profit sharing plans need to be explored.

The basic problem faced by most profit sharing plans is that they attempt to meet both the long-term, wealth-maximizing objectives of young employees with long careers ahead of them and the short-term capital preservation objectives of older employees who are about to retire. The former are quite properly not very concerned with the interim ups and downs of near-term market cycles so long as the *trend* of the fund's growth is achieving their long-term objective of matching or exceeding the appreciation of the market averages. In sharp contrast, the older employees really care only about the present market cycle and naturally fear a sharp market decline that could wipe out long years of past gains. For the young, such a decline would be only temporary; for the older employee it could be permanent. (While it is true that the profit plan payout that had been shrunk by a market drop could theoretically be immediately reinvested by the departing employee while prices are still low—enabling him to recover his investment as fast as the plan's portfolio would recover—informed observers believe that retired persons view these assets very differently from the younger worker. Since they are preparing for retirement, they tend to put their money in annuities and stocks that yield high income but appreciate slowly. Consequently, if they leave the profit sharing plan after a market drop, their funds are usually "locked in" at those low levels.)

Another problem with the omnibus, profit sharing plan is the variation in employees' dependence on it. Compare the point of view of the senior executive, with his high income, stock options, large pension, and deferred compensation agreement, with that of the widow working as a secretary to earn money to put her children through college. The former may look on the profit sharing plan as an extra "kicker," and so he favors a very aggressive investment policy. The latter, however, may be depending upon the preservation of her part of the plan as an important supplement to a modest retirement income, and so wants a conservative investment program. In formal economic terms, the utility of each marginal dollar of gain or loss will differ markedly for each of these cases. The senior executive is really only interested in a highly aggressive policy that will suit his objectives, but the secretary seeks a cautious investment program and preservation of her much needed capital. Consequently, a single purpose fund is not going to meet their diverse, often contradictory objectives.

The solution to this problem of diversity of needs and objectives among various groups of employees is quite simple, but surprisingly seldom used: the sponsoring corporation should establish several portfolios within the overall profit sharing plan, each with a different investment objective and portfolio operating policy, ranging from very aggressive to very conservative, so the participating employee can select the portfolio or combination of portfolios that will best meet his or her individual goals. Moreover, the employee should be allowed to shift the assets from one portfolio to another over time so his investment media will keep pace with changes in his financial and personal situation. An ideal group of portfolios would include the following: a bond fund, a conservative stock fund, a long-term, growth-oriented stock fund, and an aggressive, risk-taking stock fund. Each employee could then select his own mix.

The bond fund, aiming primarily at preservation of capital, would be used principally as a way for employees approaching retirement to "lock in" past gains in anticipation of leaving the plan by switching from the stock funds to the more stable bond fund and holding it until retirement. This option not only gives each individual employee a way to protect his assets against untimely market dips but also relieves the remaining portfolio assets from the obligation to minimize declines in adverse market periods which can usually be done only at the cost of also reducing relative gains in favorable markets, which would in turn contradict the appropriate goals of the younger participants in the plan.

Fortunately for pension fund managers, this duality of purpose is not a problem because the corporation usually is committed to a specific benefit payment and the employee is insulated from short-term fluctuations (declines) and so can only gain from long-term superior investment results.

So for the professional investment manager, the corporate pension fund should be the ideal client. Like the endowment fund, it is tax exempt and has a virtually perpetual life. Because current cash income exceeds current money needs, most pension funds are in the happy position of receiving more dollars to fund long-term pension obligations than are now being paid out to men and women who have already retired and are now beneficiaries, the assets of the pension fund are usually entirely free of near-term liquidity constraints and free for investment to meet long-term objectives.

While the investment policies of corporate pension funds do not have to give special attention to the interim impact of market fluctuations on the value of the portfolio, they must be directly concerned with the powerful, apparently relentless long-term trend towards higher and higher pension benefits that will be paid out of the pension fund. The confluence of several major trends—higher hourly pay, vesting and portability of benefits, earlier retirement, and the increasing acceptance of greater parity of retirement pay to working pay—all contribute to the strong upward bias to benefit payments which, when they are increased, are often also increased *retroactively*.

In other words, while the investment policy concern of the profit sharing plan executive must be with changes in the price level of the capital markets (his payment obligations are not variable), the pension executive has the opposite problem: the benefits to be paid out from his asset base are greatly variable, but are not necessarily affected by investment results. On the other hand, while the sponsoring corporation's contributions to a profit sharing plan are not variable, contributions to a pension plan can be greatly affected by changes in the rate of return realized on invested assets.

Although the steadily and rapidly rising trends of pension benefits are clearly in motion, most companies are currently funding their pensions to provide for no more than the present schedule of benefits *after* making a downward adjustment in current liability because of such actuarial factors as turnover, mortality, and particularly the expected investment income. Few if any pension executives are now anticipating the very probable large increases in capital contributions required to fund the substantially higher liabilities that will accrue in the future. Ironically, when higher benefit schedules are established, their coverage will probably be made retroactive to include work being done today.

This planning oversight has two negative consequences: it understates the size of the pension liability actually being incurred now and ultimately forces management to play "catch-up ball" with pension funding. If, however, the pension manager estimated the likely changes in benefits and translated into current terms the level of obligations expected from the present period—even though these obligations would not be formally "recognized" until a future time —corporate management would have a more realistic picture of both the trend in benefits and the related trend in funding obligations. In addition, management could evaluate more realistically the cost of fringe benefits for the present work force. When a company is obliged to make large retroactive benefit increases, it can suffer a severe reduction in reported earnings. By anticipating the rate and magnitude of future contributions, management can at least increase its annual contributions in an orderly, more "livable" way, and avoid unnecessary surprises.

The difference between present levels of funding and future levels of benefits can be made up in only two ways: higher company contributions to the capital of the pension plan, or superior long-term investment performance. Naturally, corporate management would prefer the latter. Fortunately, the pension fund is a *very* long term investment. And so good long-term investment results can make a significant difference to corporate earnings by reducing the required annual contribution to the fund. And because most pension funds do not have to rely on short-term investment results or on current income to meet benefit obligations, these funds are able to tolerate interim volatility or variance in period-to-period investment returns. They are also able to live with seemingly low levels of portfolio liquidity. Consequently, a company's top echelon should require the same bold, profit-oriented management for the pension fund as it does in the operating divisions, and should accept comparable interim risks to achieve comparable long-term profit rewards.

Given the proposition that management should take a long-term view of its fund's investment programs, the critical question becomes: How should corporate executives analyze the fund's long-term fund needs and resources? Establishing the right frame of reference here is important because senior corporate management should not be asked to vote simply *yes* or *no* to a single program. It should instead have an array of relevant options from which to select an optimum program of funding *and* investing pension assets. Once the long-term, strategic decisions are made, top management should require regular reviews of the program in the context of actual investment results, probable changes in future benefit payments, and alternative options for future funding and investing of assets.

Significant changes very clearly do take place from time to time in the pension obligations, the pension assets, and the corporation's financial situation, and management should be well prepared to adapt to these changes in an orderly manner. The importance of decisions affecting the disposition of such important assets requires well-reasoned and wisely developed methods of review and evaluation.

Two quite different formats for presenting the pension fund assets have been developed for use in making pension fund policy decisions: the "inventory of assets" approach and the "balance sheet" approach. The typical inventory of assets for a pension fund is shown in Table 7. This pension fund

TABLE 7

Inventory of assets of ABC Corporation pension fund

	Market value		Book value		
	Amount	Percent of total	Amount	Percent of total	Income
U.S. Treasury Bills	$ 354,641	0.9	$ 353,812	1.0	$ 315
U.S. government agencies	7,650	0.1	7,650	0.1	71,208
Negotiable CDs	1,592,000	3.9	1,592,000	4.7	391,876
Corporate bonds	7,851,792	19.5	7,787,609	22.8	14,000
Convertible bonds	603,875	1.0	352,450	1.0	57,026
Foreign bonds	1,111,900	2.7	1,083,628	3.2	57,026
	$11,521,858	28.1	$11,177,149	32.8	$ 534,425
Preferred stocks	217,000	1.0	308,314	0.9	9,000
Common stocks	27,186,785	68.2	21,526,067	63.2	562,245
	$27,403,785	69.2	$21,834,381	64.1	$ 571,245
Mortgages	789,423	2.0	789,639	2.3	41,374
Real estate	284,934	0.7	284,935	0.8	14,434
	$ 1,074,357	2.7	$ 1,074,574	3.1	$ 55,808
Total	$40,000,000	100.0	$34,086,104	100.0	$1,161,478

presentation format is not really very useful because it ignores the enormous, growing liabilities for which these assets
have been accumulated, and it does not match current assets
with current liabilities or long-term assets with long-term
liabilities. The balance sheet format shown in Table 8 is far
more relevant and useful because it enables management to
analyze both the liabilities and the assets in a rational way
and determine which are relatively current and which are long
term.

A "business cycle" in the investment field is longer than
the 12 months of the usual corporate accounting convention.
Therefore, "current" liabilities should be considered to be
those amounts which the fund is obligated to pay in less time
than it would realistically take to make prudent use of them
in long-term investments. Thus, for example, if you need $1
million in 18 months to meet a fixed commitment, it would be
unwise to "risk" these funds in common stocks which might
experience a bear market between now and then. These liabilities should be matched by "current" assets, in the form of
highly marketable securities that will provide a suitable primary liquid reserve, plus current income from investments.
In the example shown in Table 8, I have used two years as
an appropriate measure of the "current" period for an invested pension fund because for investment purposes, two
years is a relatively short time period and is closer to "current" than would be a conventional 12-month period.

Balancing current liabilities with truly current assets and
long-term liabilities with long-term assets not only helps
make sure that all current and intermediate liabilities can
be met from liquid reserves, but also frees long-term assets
from undue concern with either liquidity or the superficial
"risk" of short-term market value fluctuations. As a result,
both corporate managers and investment managers can concentrate on achieving maximum long-term returns with these

TABLE 8

Balance sheet of ABC Corporation pension fund

ASSETS

Current assets, or primary reserve fund:
Money-market instruments
U.S. government issues
High-grade corporate bonds
Total primary reserve .... $ 2,000,000

Immediate assets, or secondary reserve fund:
Money-market instruments
Corporate bonds
Convertible bonds
Convertible preferred stocks
Common stocks 6,000,000
Total secondary reserve .... $ 8,000,000
Total current and intermediate assets

Long-term assets, or variable return fund:
Corporate bonds with warrants
Low-grade corporate bonds
Common stocks
Real estate
Oil royalties
Mortgages
Sale-leasebacks
Private placements
Venture capital
Total long-term assets 32,000,000
Total assets $40,000,000

LIABILITIES

Current liabilities:
Accrued benefits—retired employees' current portion (payable within 2 years) $ 2,000,000

Intermediate liabilities:
Accrued benefits—retired employees (payable in 2–5 years) 4,000,000
Accrued benefits—active and terminated vested employees retiring within 5 years (payable within 5 years) 2,000,000
Total current and intermediate liabilities .... $ 8,000,000

Long-term liabilities:
Accrued, vested benefits—active and terminated employees (payable after 5 years) 10,000,000
Accrued, nonvested benefits—active employees (payable after 5 years) 18,000,000
Surplus (deficit) 4,000,000
Total liabilities and surplus $40,000,000

long-term funds. The importance of separating investment objectives can hardly be overstated. Most pension funds are heavily invested in listed stocks and high-grade bonds, and so are highly liquid. They have not ventured into less liquid, but often higher yielding investments such as real estate, oil and gas production payments, and mortgages, so these funds may well be paying a penalty in lower returns to obtain something they do not need: nearly total liquidity.

Management must know where it is headed in order to make wise decisions about funding the pension program and investing its assets. By taking the time and care to estimate the changes that are likely to take place in each of the principal factors in what might be called the "pension fund equation," management can develop a model for present and future funding obligations and for benefit payment liabilities. This can be an important planning tool in two vital areas of pension finance: setting investment objectives and policies that are suited to the mission of the fund, and accruing corporate contributions to the fund in an orderly manner.

The pension fund equation or model combines inputs from three different groups: investment managers, corporate managers responsible for wage and salary administrations, and consulting actuaries. Unfortunately, these groups usually are not brought close together, with the result that in most cases the senior executives responsible for pension policies fail to get a comprehensive forecast or plan. Here are the main elements needed for a comprehensive pension plan, listed according to the best source for each:

From investment managers should come the expected rate of return over the next 12 months from highly marketable, fixed-income securities held in the primary reserve portion of the fund; and also the cash and noncash returns, as well as probable variability of each part of total return expected over the next several years for each of these types of possible investment: common stocks (cyclical, steady-growth, high-growth, and special-situation groups), corporate bonds, bonds with equity kickers or convertibility, mortgages, real estate developments, plant and equipment leases, private debt placements, and natural resource production payments and royalties.

From wage and salary administrators should come careful estimates for each of the next several years of changes in wage and salary levels, in vesting and portability of benefits, in the number and pay-grade mix of employees, in the ratio of pension pay to working pay, and in either or both voluntary and mandatory early retirement, plus the impact of possible changes in pension regulation or in methods of integrating with social security. (Some of these elements can best be obtained from, or in cooperation with, actuaries.)

From consulting actuaries should come projections of the impact of shifts in the age mix of employees, calculations of mortality and disability effects on benefit payments, estimates of the impact of employee turnover, and a long-term average rate-of-return assumption based on experience of many comparably managed funds of a similar size.

Armed with estimates for each of these elements, management can proceed to determine its own corporation's pension fund equation, which is the most probable pattern combining these diverse cost and revenue factors. From these calculations management can project the annual level of benefit payments, the corporation's annual funding obligations over the next several years, and the degree of liquidity necessary to ensure the fund's ability to meet current and intermediate benefit obligations.

Management will also want an analysis of how changes in each element might affect the results of the "most probable" run-through of the pension fund equation. This "sensitivity analysis" will enable management to test how alternative assumptions about the elements of the equation would affect the benefits, obligations, and the funding requirements. An important benefit of the analysis is its help in identifying which elements are most influential so that management can focus its efforts on these high-leverage elements. Another benefit easily derived from the analysis is a high-medium-low type of projection of money flows into and out of the pension fund. This can be very useful in estimating the probable and potential liquidity needs over the next several years and for setting proper limits on primary and secondary liquidity reserves which protect the long-term investment program from "current" considerations.

While most pension funds are now experiencing a positive net cash flow and so are not concerned about portfolio liquidity, this happy state of affairs will not last forever. So every pension executive should have a rational "distant early warning system" to protect his fund (and his financial statement) from an unanticipated liquidity squeeze. The major benefit of projecting the probable pension fund "flow of funds" is in showing senior management what the long-run future holds. Many an otherwise sophisticated financial manager, having neglected to forecast realistically the *future* liabilities and *future* assets of his pension fund, is not sufficiently progressive in programming either the funding or the investing of pension assets to meet the surging expansion of long-term liabilities.

The primary importance of careful pension fund projections is not just to protect against a sudden liquidity crisis but to provide the basis for developing and implementing a sound long-term pension strategy that will respond appropriately to the impressive size of pension assets, their burgeoning growth, and the rapidly changing demands being made on these assets.

Long-range strategic planning must become standard procedure in pension fund administration. This is a senior management responsibility that should not be passively delegated to outsiders who are prepared to deal with only part of the problem. Although actuaries can help quantify and project the annual dollar consequences of various changes in pension benefits, and investment managers can help increase the average rate of return on invested pension fund assets, only senior corporate management knows enough about the future of the company and its compensation philosophy to lay out the basic elements of an effective pension strategy. The tradeoff between higher company contributions and higher investment returns is essentially a management-stockholder problem because the employees are virtually guaranteed against loss if investment results are inferior: the company will simply have to put up more money. So, once the benefit payments schedule has been determined, the funding and operation of the pension fund is essentially a problem of long-term financial management.

It would be improper and incorrect in setting financial policy for pension funds to view pension expenditures as a short-term or current operating cost; they are, quite the contrary, long-term capital investments. When the corporation's senior management transfers a large chunk of capital from the treasury *irrevocably* into the separate legal entity of the pension fund, it should insist that this capital earn at least as high a rate of return as capital invested in other parts of the corporation. Otherwise, the transfer should not be made or at least should be made only reluctantly, because it directly harms the shareholders to divert scarce investment capital to inferior returns.

In setting basic investment policies, the corporation's directors should pursue essentially the same goals in essentially the same way as has already been developed for trustees of endowment funds, because they are concerned with essentially the same kind of capital with essentially the same mission—

both are tax exempt and both finance very long term programs. The only major difference, other than legal requirements that may be imposed, is that corporations can probably accept greater volatility risk in their pension funds than universities can accept in their endowment funds because if the total return of the endowment falls, even for only a brief period, the institution's operating budget may be thrown into acute jeopardy. On the other hand, a profitable corporation can replenish an unlikely investment loss and, as noted above, the typical pension fund has no near-term cash liquidity problems.

As a consequence of the corporation's freedom from excessive concern with adverse short-term investment results and its opportunity to benefit from long-term investment profits, management should insist upon as bold and profit-oriented pension management as it requires in other divisions of the corporation, and should accept comparable interim risks to achieve comparable long-term profit rewards. In other words, the senior management of a corporation should look at its pension fund as a competitive user of capital to be rigorously compared to the operating divisions that can also use that corporate resource. The long-term benefit of superior pension fund performance to the corporation can be quite substantial: the annual costs of meeting pension obligations can be reduced; benefits paid to employees can be increased; and less capital need be diverted from the company's primary business purpose.

Moreover, it is the corporation—its earnings and its capital —that will feel the brunt of the force with which rising pension benefits will affect corporate finance, once the easy cushion of inflating actuarial assumptions is used up. That time is quite close when pension contributions will have to be made exclusively in hard cash dollars rather than to some degree in the soft currency of changing assumed rates of return.

By anticipating the magnitude and timing of that change through careful long-range pension planning, corporate financial executives can absorb these changes in an orderly manner.

Pension assets and funding are too important to business, to employees, and even to our national goals to be handled on an *ad hoc* basis with only near-term planning horizons. Fulfillment of corporate and fiduciary responsibility over the decades ahead will require both careful financial planning and vigorous investment management to make pension assets the truly productive capital they can and should be.

19

The individual as client

The INDIVIDUAL INVESTOR is obsolete. As in any other competitive field in which professionals are dominant, the amateur investor is not likely to enjoy significant success. He does not have the information resources, the supporting staff of analysts and traders, the "quick response capability," or the on-line experience of the many professional investors who are active in the securities markets as his direct competitors. He is not competitive and should not try to compete. Fortunately, he has a simple and easily implemented alternative: he can join 'em.

Professional investment managers seldom charge their clients more than a 1 percent management fee. Most charge less. In a real sense, this fee can be looked upon as an insurance premium, a *casualty* insurance premium with the investment manager's main role being to protect the individual—and his capital—from himself. This may sound patronizing, and perhaps it is, but even the most casual observer of individual investors, particularly those who are also doctors, lawyers, and businessmen, will have noticed game and gaming terms used to describe their investments: "I really hit one with XYZ," "a sure double," "a good tip," "he has a friend whose brother-in-law is close to this one," "I'm doubling up on this one," "an excellent speculation." At a race track or a casino this could be harmless enough because it would be big talk about relatively small amounts. But with investment portfolios, the amateurs' chatter is all too often about their entire family savings for education, retirement, a new house, and other major objectives that warrant more serious consideration.

One of the principal problems with amateur investors is that they do not know the facts. If they knew what their actual investment results have been, most would immediately join the search for good professional management. At least three factors combine to delude most individual investors. First, money is "put into" the market or "taken out of" the market at irregular times with the result that "time-weighted" average rates of return are quite difficult to calculate. And so accurate measures of actual performance do not confront the merry amateur with grim reality.

Second, when real money is "put into" the market, it becomes curiously unreal. An odd euphoria overcomes the investor. His assets are no longer a store of real buying power, but rather a list of stocks like poker chips, and Mister Chance soon becomes his partner. His feelings about the market and his role as an investor might be far more sober if he followed the simple practice of at least once each year "cashing in his chips" for real money and spending half an hour in his banker's vault contemplating a stack of one dollar bills equal to his invested wealth. This confrontation with reality might well persuade him to pursue another path toward investment success.

The third factor is the self-delusion or self-indulgence

which allows the amateur to increase his "profits" by thinking he paid less than he really paid for individual stocks and believing he sold them for more than was actually the case. This enlarged profit-per-trade is often magnified again by falsely believing that he bought more of the "winners" and less of the "losers" than are actually shown on his broker's transaction slips. The saddest pretense is to measure the value of "winners" in terms of the current market price while pretending that the price drop of "losers" is only temporary and that their original purchase cost is their real current value. ("It'll come back.") Again, the only thing wrong with this very human foolishness is that the amounts of money involved can be very large (men who have never bet $50 on a 50–50 toss of a coin will "invest" $5,000 on a "good tip" with 50–1 odds against them).

While arguing that investors should be more conscious of the fact that their investments represent very real money, it is equally important to recognize that invested capital *is only money*. Too many investors attach elaborate sentimental importance to individual holdings, particularly those that happen to have appreciated substantially or were received as gifts or bequests. While in some cases these gifts were made with the understanding that they would thereafter be held indefinitely, more often the gift was intended only as a transfer of wealth and the particular shares involved were merely incidental. By and large, investors would put themselves in a better position if they would try diligently to think of their securities in cold objective terms. It is real money; but it is only money. As 'Adam Smith' so aptly phrased it, "The stock does not know you own it."

Another problem individual investors have is their great reluctance to pay taxes on investment profits. Most investors have suffered substantial losses at one time or another because they held onto a stock they would have sold at far higher prices except for their feeling of being locked in by the taxes they would have been assessed on the realized profit. Often, in retrospect, this was not wise. The investor who really seeks to maximize his long-term profits must be prepared to incur and pay the taxes involved. The problem most investors have with taxes is that they believe the tax incurred in selling a profitable stock should be fully recovered within one or two years or else their capital should not be switched from the old stock to a new stock. They view the problem this way: "I paid $50 for ABC and it's now worth $100 so my tax would be $15 (30 percent of $50 gain) which leaves me only $85 to reinvest in XYZ. This means XYZ has to go up at least 20 percent or $15 *more* than ABC does for me to come out even before year-end tax time. I don't think the odds on that are very good so I'll hold onto my ABC." The errors in this line of reasoning are at least two: the investor who holds ABC is not escaping the tax, he is only deferring it; and the time period within which the tax is to be "recovered" should not be just one year, but several years. For example, if five years are allowed for full tax recovery, then a 4 percent higher annual gain for XYZ over ABC will do the job very nicely. Putting taxes in the proper time dimension greatly reduces their inhibiting emotional effect, but the economic reality is that the tax is only being postponed. If a stock should be sold for any good *investment* reason, it should never be held for any *tax* reason. Stock price dips cut into profits faster and deeper than taxes. At least taxes don't ever take *all* the profit. In sum, individual investors should ignore taxes because over the long run, the really heavy cost of taxes comes not from paying the taxes, but from investors making bad investment decisions just "for tax reasons."

Briefly then, the professionals have many important operating advantages over the amateurs; the amateur usually burdens himself with special problems including a phobia of

paying taxes, false sentimentality, and unreal, romantic per-
ceptions of his investment results by which he deludes himself
into feeling he is doing far better on his own than he is. All
this even though the best professionals offer their best services to the willing amateur at what must be considered a
modest fee relative to the economic advantages he should
achieve *over the long term with superior professional management.*

Most individual investors will face an honest trauma when
turning their investment affairs over to a professional. In
plain fact, most investors find this step so disconcerting that
they have avoided taking it altogether. On the other hand,
each year some individuals make sound decisions about professional management and can expect to profit from the consequences. Still others fall between the two: they make the
critical decision, but make it badly. Usually they go to a good
friend instead of to a good investor. The results can and often
do wreck both friendship and portfolio. Perhaps it is arbitrary, but a good rule would be this one: Never try to make
an investment manager of your friend; never try to make a
friend of your investment manager. Investments should be
a strictly-for-business matter.

The investment field is filled with nice guys who give well-
intended but inferior advice. Their social strengths can't
really compensate for their business weakness. The individual
investor who feels drawn to an investment adviser who is
strong on "bedside manner" should force himself to remember that it is *his* money and that the hidden costs of inferior
results can run very, very high. Put it this way: the investment manager who builds his business on grace and charm
and a keen interest in you (and many, many, many others)
as a prospective client is giving short shrift to the tough work
of doing a superior job of making money with money in the
investment arena.

The second mistake individual investors make is also very human; they insist upon having their own investment account. They'll have no part of a mutual fund or other pooled portfolio. This is really too bad because it virtually dooms them to inferior results unless their assets comfortably exceed $1 million. Even millionaires would be better off economically if they invested in mutual funds—and many millionaires do.

The reason most individuals should buy into mutual funds or the like is quite simple. First, a small account with separate management is uneconomic to a good investment manager, so he can only afford the time to make an occasional cursory review of these portfolios while he is spending several hours every day working to advance the portfolio of his best and most profitable clients. At least one of these "best accounts" is likely to be a mutual fund which he manages as a showpiece to attract more new business. The small to medium size individual account that is invested in that fund will automatically get "best account" treatment. Another advantage of investing via mutual funds or joint trust accounts is that even a modest investor can diversify his managers at virtually no extra cost by investing in several different pooled portfolios. Again, by comparing the actual results achieved in one such fund vis-à-vis the others, he can relatively easily "manage the managers." A manager who begins to fall short of the group will show up quite quickly and clearly and remedial action can be taken by the investor early rather than too late.

Selecting the specific managers for an individual's portfolio is not really as hard as it looks to the typical individual who recognizes he does not know very much about the investment management business. The method is very simple and can prove both interesting and enjoyable. Ask around. Ask people who are in the investment field the direct question: "If you were me, which two or three investment managers would you pick *for the long term* and why?" Then research those who seem high on your composite list. If you decide to interview a few of these managers, be sure to ask *them* the same question about *other* money managers. In a few weeks, your choices should be narrowed down to a good group of managers. Then, since there is no one perfect manager for your account, pick three to five from the group and invest in their mutual funds. Then, at least once every two years, go through the same process all over again with special attention to significant changes in the personal and business lives of these chosen managers which might hurt their future performance on your behalf. If, after investigation, you would feel more confident by making one or more changes in your management line-up, by all means do so promptly. Remember, you are still making investment decisions; they are much more important decisions than the ones you made when you were picking individual stocks.

Most individual investors approach the selection of an investment manager by asking themselves, "How much do I want to *make* from my investments?" Naturally enough, they ask the prospective managers "How much can I expect to make with you as my manager?" These individuals would do better to ask themselves "How much am I willing to *lose?*" and to ask the prospective manager "How much should I be prepared to lose in the short run to achieve my goals over the long run?" In other words, aiming for higher average returns over the long run axiomatically involves accepting greater fluctuations—up *and* down—in the short run. Unless these fluctuations can be lived with comfortably, the investor's aim should not be set so high.

A final note: individual investors should make thoughtful financial plans, preferably once each year, to be sure that their action program is appropriate to their individual goals and priorities. They should also review quite carefully where they are each year to be sure their hopes and expectations are realistic. Even for the individual of moderate wealth, investment management is serious business, and warrants careful attention.

In selecting a group of investment managers, the individual investor may well find that he does not think of his capital as one large account with several purposes (retirement, education, bequests, and others) but rather as several different funds, each with its own purpose. In this latter case, the investor may be wise to divide the total capital into segments with different investment objectives such as: liquid funds for vacations, art purchases, and the like; moderate growth, blue chip fund for children's education; very aggressive fund for a possible new house or bigger gifts to alma mater; moderately aggressive stock fund for use in retirement; and so forth. This process of splitting off sub-accounts can easily be overdone, but it can help considerably to insulate the bulk of one's capital from those special considerations that can realistically be met by a fraction of the whole.

One specific suggestion that can relieve much of the human pressure to make the sort of mistakes outlined earlier in this chapter is to keep a few thousand dollars aside for your own speculations on tips and concepts that compel you to take some sort of action, foolish as it may be. This "gambler's allowance" may be expensive, but it is far cheaper than swinging with all your capital.

This chapter has been devoted to the thesis that the individual investor should hire good professional management for his capital. Clearly, this approach does not have as much fun and excitement (or pathos and tragedy) as doing it oneself. As a result, few who read this sober advice will accept it for themselves, which will assure the professional investors of at least some amateur competition and so will continue to give professionals a good chance of beating the averages.

20

The impact of
institutional investing
on corporations
and capital markets

INSTITUTIONAL INVESTING dominates the investment arena.
More than half of all transactions on the stock exchanges are
executed for professional investors and this share of market
seems to be rising inexorably. And more than one third of the
shares of our nation's corporations are already owned by
institutions investing other peoples' money. More impressive
than the sheer size of the institutions is the speed with which
they have grown and are still growing. This chapter describes
some of the ways in which institutional investing has made its
impact felt by corporations and capital markets, and suggests
some of the public policy issues that result.

The impact of institutional investing on the capital markets
has been truly revolutionary, and it would be naive to assume
that the changes of the seventies will be any less exciting and

significant than those of the sixties. Obviously, the volume of
trading on the exchanges has mushroomed with daily average
trading volume two and three times the average of just a decade ago. More impressive than the simple growth in unit
volume has been a change in the nature of stock transactions.

Block trading—execution of purchase and sale orders of
10,000 or more shares in a single transaction—has become
really big business. In recent years, transactions of 50,000
and 100,000 shares have become commonplace. Several transactions of over one million shares have literally changed
the scale of most imaginations in Wall Street. More importantly, large block trades have become a regular feature of
the equity markets and have fundamentally changed the nature and structure of our nation's exchanges.

The classic description of the New York Stock Exchange as
a perfect auction market with both buyers and sellers openly
bidding with each other is as passé as the idea that the specialist on the floor of the exchange can provide "continuous
markets" and smooth out the "ripples" in prices caused by
large irregularities in buying and selling interests. The specialist who could buy 1,000 or even 10,000 shares is simply
unable to cope with the capital required to digest block transactions of 100,000 or 500,000 shares—nor can such volume
be absorbed readily by the classic auction market still conducted on the exchange floor for investors who want to buy or
sell 100 or less shares.

Today, the market for large transactions between institutions is *not* an auction, is *not* conducted on or even very near
the exchange floor, and is *not* made public until after the
transactions are fully settled as to amount and price. Block
trades are privately negotiated transactions. They do not depend to any substantial degree upon either the facilities or
the procedures of the stock exchanges. As a result of this remarkable difference between the new institutional transac-

tions and the customary individual transactions, the regular exchanges no longer have full control over trading in the shares they list. This is because such transactions can be executed on regional exchanges which dually list the stocks involved or can be executed in the so-called third market which operates on an over-the-counter basis. With the recent automation of the over-the counter markets, another challenger is in the lists against the traditional exchanges. The primacy of the New York and American Stock Exchanges is being challenged because institutional investors have different needs than individual investors and are pressing inevitably for changes that will meet their new needs.

Block trading is truly the "new underwriting" when the executing broker acts as principal as well as agent and commits his own capital—often several millions of dollars at a time—to "round out" the buy side of a large block trade or to buy all by himself a large volume of shares that a client wants to sell quickly at a time when no substantial buyers are known. The several brokerage firms that are regularly putting large amounts of their capital at risk to execute mammoth block transactions provide a new dimension of wholesale liquidity to the equity markets that has become essential because of the growth of the investment institutions and their needs for new services.

Institutional block trading may someday break up the traditional monopoly in stock underwriting. Although the practice has not yet been adopted on a significant scale, the development of a viable block trading market could easily displace the traditional method of underwriting secondary and primary offerings of shares in issues widely held by institutions. In point of fact, in the last decade very few stock underwritings of seasoned companies have been larger than the larger block trades. In other words, block trading firms and facilities could handle the large volume distributions that historically depended upon underwriting firms and facilities. Moreover, the mutual funds which once used secondary offerings to dispose of large holdings now almost exclusively use block trades to effect such sales, because they are faster, easier, and far less expensive. A privately negotiated block market sale of 300,000 shares of a $50 stock may involve a discount of 50 cents to a dollar and a 20-cent commission to the broker; and it will usually be arranged and completed in but one or two days. In contrast, an underwriting or a secondary distribution can take weeks, would involve two or three extra commissions to participating brokers, and during these prolonged preparations the stock being sold might easily suffer a price discount of several dollars. These time and money costs are not justified, so over time the institutionally oriented block market may well gain a significant share of traditional underwriting business.

Another way in which institutional investors have had an important impact on the markets has followed from their needs for information services. A whole new group of brokerage firms have developed in response to this need and the profits that could be earned by serving the institutions' information requirements. (Increasingly, these new "institutional" firms—and the "institutional" departments created within older and more traditional firms—have taken leadership in the brokerage field.) The efforts of these institutional brokers and their clients have resulted in the creation of an extraordinary information system over which an enormous volume of fact and opinion is transmitted with remarkable speed throughout the country and abroad.

Since institutional investors react swiftly—and on a big-volume scale—to changes in expectations, stock prices are quickly adjusted to the new perceived reality. Several years ago, in contrast, days, weeks, and even months would pass before a stock would have "found its new level." More importantly, the market has fewer discontinuities or imbalances between the price of one stock and the prices of other stocks. Prices are smoother or more homogeneous because institutional investors are not only able to deal comfortably in finer shades of difference between seemingly diverse groups of stocks, but also have created a richer liquidity in the market as a whole. Some casual observers have argued that institutions disrupt the market by "dumping" stocks, but closer study would show that it is not that the amount of price change has increased so much as the speed with which it occurs has increased. Declines that formerly took several months now occur in minutes—a swifter response to the same adverse developments. In other words, the stock market is more nearly a "perfect" market. (It is interesting to note how often comment is made when a stock's price drops quickly and how seldom comment is made when a stock's price jumps up due to the activity of institutional investors.)

In brief, then, the impact of institutional investing on the stock market has resulted in new brokerage firms providing new kinds of services in new ways to meet new demands from a newly predominant group of clients. It bears repeating that the full consequences of this impact have not yet been seen.

The impact of investment institutions upon corporations has been at least as dramatic and substantive as their impact on the stock market. The impact of professional investors on corporate management comes in two areas: liquidity and information. The impact of the information requirements of institutional investors has caused a dramatic increase in the number and quality of investment analysts digging for new and better information. In many cases, these analysts are recognized by corporate executives in the industries they "follow" as the best informed experts on important developments in and out of the industry that will affect its future. Beyond this, however, analysts representing institutions directly or indirectly seldom will accept passively the party line from management. They probe for inconsistency. They require documentation and substantiation. They cite conflicting evidence or contradictory views. And they offer constructive suggestions on a wide range of issues with which management must deal. In brief, the well-informed and inquisitive investment analyst often performs the vital and influential role usually expected of a company's directors who, by contrast, often are less current on critical factors and less deeply immersed in the investors' viewpoint. Although meetings between top analysts and top management are seldom relaxed and jovial, time and again busy executives agree that these meetings are an important part of their decision-making apparatus and have had a significant influence on actual decisions made.

In addition to the pursuit of information, institutional investors have influenced corporations through the phenomenal liquidity which has developed to accommodate their large block transactions. This impact has been most obvious in mergers. The acceptability of merger terms by a few institutions with large holdings can virtually guarantee a deal, while dissatisfaction on their part can prohibit consummation. When a tender offer is accepted by a few major institutions, the shares tendered by them can give the tendering corporation a vital advantage in executing its program. On the other hand, if institutional holders of the tendering company's stock do not like proposed merger terms and begin liquidating their holdings, the share price may drop enough to break up the merger before it gets far advanced. Whether for good or for ill, the rise of conglomerate acquisition companies in the late 1960s was perhaps the fullest expression of the impact on corporations of the new liquidity created by and for institutional investors who were and are sized on the same scale as our nation's giant corporations.

An important albeit intangible result of both the liquidity and the information of institutional investors is the attention and determination of senior managements of large corporations to increase productivity of corporate assets. In some cases this movement has taken the form of an acquisition of a dormant corporation by a more aggressive management. In other cases, sleepy managements have been aroused by fear of what might happen to them if they did not more effectively serve investor interests and expectations. And unfortunately in some cases, short-term investor profits have sometimes been made at a real cost to the long-term well-being of hastily merged companies. But in most cases, senior management has simply recognized more fully than before that investor-owners have an important and legitimate right to be well represented in the major decisions and policies of the corporations in which they hold shares. Those managers who refuse to accept this proposition should realize that they court trouble with dissatisfied institutional investors.

In part because of their impact on corporations and capital markets and in part because of their sheer size and rapid growth, investment institutions are raising a series of important public policy issues. Size alone makes investment institutions politically relevant because they are axiomatically affected with the public interest. And yet, since these massive aggregations of capital are a relatively recent phenomenon— they were wholly without precedent 25 years ago and only recently have come to be a primary force in our investment economy—few of the public policy issues have been resolved. So, in concluding this book it seems fitting to focus briefly upon some of the issues created by institutional investing which call for resolution in the near future.

- Should the investment profits of pension and profit sharing funds, particularly short-term "trading profits," continue to receive tax-exempt status or should such status be limited to truly long term, passive investments?

- Should commercial banks be allowed to continue to operate trust departments or is there a conflict of interest between their creditor and investor roles?
- Should mutual funds controlled by management companies be allowed to use portfolio commissions to motivate dealers to sell their shares? Should mutual funds be "mutualized"? How "independent" should directors of mutual funds be in their dealings with the management company?
- Does the development of a fast and effective information network among institutions and brokers mean that the institutions have access to and use nonpublic or "insider" information? If so, what should be done about it?
- Do institutional investors operate informally in pools and thereby manipulate stock prices?
- Should institutional investors continue to be generally passive investors in corporations or should they actively seek seats on boards of directors, solicit proxies, and take a strong hand in selecting operating management and setting corporate policy?
- Should institutions be allowed to join the principal stock exchanges? If so, on what terms? And what defines an "institution"?
- Should brokers be allowed to offer investment management services to clients for a fee in competition with non-member institutions?
- Do institutions speculate in improper ways? If so, what action can or should be taken? And by whom?
- Should all publicly owned corporations be required to make full disclosure of all pertinent and current information (as is done in a prospectus) and be required to do so at least once each year?

- Is the SEC properly organized and financed to serve its proper role in modern times? What changes are needed?
- Should banks be allowed to make "take over" loans to corporations and accept as collateral the shares acquired in the tender offer?
- Should pension funds be required to invest part of their assets in socially desirable investments such as home mortgages?
- Should the stock exchanges be managed by their members or by a publicly appointed governing board?
- Have corporate managers put too much emphasis on short-term financial measures of their business success as a result of institutional investor pressures for regular and near-term per share earnings gains?

Institutional investing has been a dramatic and powerful phenomenon. It is an exciting new kind of business. And it will surely change our nation's business and financial structure in the years ahead. This powerful new force can and should be harnessed for the greatest public good. To achieve this goal will require a sense of high purpose and professionalism. The questions of public policy posed in this chapter should be answered carefully, thoughtfully, and swiftly.

Index

237

This book has been set in 12 point and 11 point Bodoni Book, leaded 3 points. Chapter numbers are in 30 point Corvinus Medium and chapter titles are in 24 point Corvinus Medium. The size of the type page is 24 by 44½ picas.